D0961861

UNKNOWN BUT KNOWN

UNKNOWN
BUT KNOWN

My Adventure into
the Meditative Dimension

by Arthur Ford

HARPER & ROW, PUBLISHERS

NEW YORK, EVANSTON, AND LONDON

1817

To my friends
Of Spiritual Frontiers Fellowship

Contents

Acknowledgments

I here express my appreciation to Eugene Exman for his inspiration and counsel, to Jerome Ellison for his editorial guidance, to the editors of *Gateway* magazine for their co-operation in sharing experiences also reported in that magazine, to my many friends of Spiritual Frontiers Fellowship and my other visitors who have obligingly made available transcripts of their sittings, and, as always, to my co-worker Fletcher.

ARTHUR FORD

Philadelphia
June, 1968

On the Shore

1

This book is written to invite humanity to a discovery of its own psychic potential; to suggest exploration of dimensions so vast that any probing of physical space shrinks by comparison; to sketch in outline such borderlands of this dimension as have already been tentatively mapped.

Forty years ago I discovered, to my complete consternation, that I had mediumistic powers. These asserted themselves to such an extent that there was nothing for it but what Otto Rank has called "the volitional affirmative of the obligatory"—if you're stuck with something, try to make the best of it. Though it turned topsy-turvy my habitual ways of thinking about things, though it made hash of my carefully laid plans for what I was going to do with my life, I was swept willy-nilly into a career of mediumship.

Over the years my imposed vocation has brought many rewards, not the least of which is a day-to-day acquaintance with things most people of our time would consider extraordinary.

Only the other day, three Vietnam veterans from Fort Bragg came to see me. They were just out of an army hospital. All had survived very serious wounds. They told me of their experiences.

There had been six American soldiers in a Vietnam dugout when an enemy artillery shell struck. Three of the soldiers had been killed instantly, their bodies so hideously scrambled that it required only a glance to see that the survival of any one of them was utterly impossible. The other three were so seriously wounded physically that only prompt medical attention could save them. They were stunned by the shell's concussion. In this condition, *all three* saw the body of one of their dead comrades pull itself together and stand erect. They distinctly heard his voice say, "I will die but you will be saved." The body then seemed to return to its disintegrated condition. Until later, when they were able to compare experiences, each of the three had assumed that he had been dazed by the explosion and was hallucinating.

Within minutes a helicopter rescue crew arrived and took the three survivors to a field hospital, saving their lives. The 'copter pilot explained how he happened to arrive so promptly: "I was cruising at about three thousand feet when I heard a loud voice at my ear: 'There are three wounded men in a dugout directly under you. Pick them up.' I am accustomed to obeying orders. I dropped straight down. When I was close to the ground I saw the men, landed, and picked them up."

Let us consider what this episode—only one of a great many like it—implies: First, the existence of some kind of functioning body besides the physical one. Second, communication between people considered dead and people who are living. Third, a driving desire for loving service, of such force that it can transcend physical circumstances usually considered immutable.

How can such a thing happen? That it did happen, despite the absence of laboratory conditions of observation, cannot reasonably be questioned. We know it happened, not only because of the unassailable veracity of those who reported it, but because it falls solidly within a category of things that happen regularly, sometimes under conditions where objective verification is possible. It belongs in a class of events that have been occurring since man's first arrival on earth and will recur innumerable times. Some, including myself, consider them part of the natural law governing man's psychophysical nature. Parapsychologists call these cases "moment-of-death stress phenomena," a category delineated by a great body of evidence of both the subjective and objective kinds.

Why, if such dramatic things happen so often, do so few people in our time really believe they happen at all? It is just this question, and those other questions that cluster so closely about this central one, that this book undertakes to answer. What is the source of our obstinate and almost universal disbelief? Whose interests are served by routinely denying what is routinely demonstrated? What great fear inhibits us from accepting the truths that would liberate man into a new and higher level of consciousness? What keeps us from exploring the great ocean on whose shore we stand? What stops us from moving bravely and candidly into the meditative dimension? Because the circumstances of my life have thrust me against them in a way that has made them inescapable, I have been obliged to give long consideration to these questions. To some of them I have answers.

I am by no means alone in my feeling that the prevailing materialist view of the universe restricts and falsifies our understanding of reality. At one point in my life I had a deep experience with drugs, and I have concluded that the drug route ends in a blind alley. However, the drive that sets so many young feet on the path to experience in a new dimension is, though in the case of drug use misdirected, authentic, essential to our ultimate realization of our humanity. It is a reaching toward a new level of being, material and non-material, physical and psychic, through which our too-materialist lives may be restored to balance. It is an intense and, I believe, evolutionary effort of man to expand his consciousness into a dimension by comparison with which the reaches of space exploration shrink to baseball size. This same spiritual vitamin is also sought, often with real success, in the new interest of young people in drugless meditation. It is certainly the theme of Spiritual Frontiers Fellowship, the society of inner exploration that has absorbed so much of my own interest and effort in recent years.

Although even as a small boy I always seemed to have a pretty clear notion of what people around me were thinking, I assumed everybody had such insights and felt myself in no way "different." I had no experiences I had to put down as clearly "psychic" until I was twenty-two years old. I was born in Titusville, Florida—population three hundred—and spent my boyhood in Fort Pierce in the same state. My mother, though *very* Baptist, allowed me to be baptized in the church of my father, who was a steamboat captain and one of those ardent non-church-attending Episcopalians. A good deal of my boyhood was centered around the Baptist Church. I was playing the piano at young people's meetings at twelve, and it was more or less taken for granted that I'd go into the ministry. I was read out of the Baptist Church when I was sixteen, however, because of certain Unitarian notions which, in the opinion of my elders, had corrupted my Baptist faith. In 1917 I joined the Christian Church and enrolled at Transylvania University in Lexington, Kentucky. When America entered World War I, I joined the army and was sent to Camp Grant. It was here that my first major psychic experience came upon me.

During the peak of the 1918 influenza epidemic several Camp Grant soldiers died of the disease every night. One morning I awoke with the names of those who had died in camp during the night written plain before my eyes. When units of my division were sent into combat in France (I was not sent overseas) I dreamed—with infallible correctness —the casualty lists before they were published.

I was greatly disturbed by this new and unasked "gift." When I returned to Transylvania in 1919 I sought the help of a friendly and learned professor of psychology. During the following years, under his guidance, I learned most of what was then known about parapsychology. Most of this was recorded in the transactions of the Society for Psychical Research of Great Britain (these archives remain an invaluable source of information). Meanwhile I continued my preparation for the ministry. I was ordained when I was twenty-five years old. After serving a Kentucky parish I was briefly and unsatisfactorily married, then divorced. My mediumship, by this time, had taken over more and more of my life. In 1924 I went to New York, where I found myself much in demand for platform appearances as a lecturer and demonstrator of psychic phenomena.

When I was twenty-seven, and just beginning to gain enough command of my psychic resources so I felt some assurance of being able to manage seances and platform appearances with some regularity of success, I acquired a very important partner in my work. It happened quietly, abruptly, without preliminaries, indeed without my knowing it, since I was in trance at the time and I never remember anything from the trance state, which in my case resembles dreamless sleep. In one of my seances during this period a discarnate personality identifying himself simply as "Fletcher" announced that henceforth he would function as my permanent partner on the unseen plane. In all seances since that time Fletcher has invariably come on first, and opened proceedings by introducing himself. Then he acts as master of ceremonies, preparing the way for whatever discarnate guests may have been attracted to the particular sitting.

During a number of seances of this period Fletcher dropped bits of information about himself. These were passed on to me until finally I came to know quite a bit about my invisible partner. It turned out that Fletcher had been one of the French Canadian youngsters (sitters tell me he still speaks with a French accent) who lived across the river from my boyhood home in Florida. His family later moved to Canada. He had been drafted in World War I and killed in action. So that everything might be verified, he gave names and addresses of his "earthside" family and details of his army units and military record. That there had indeed been such a person, matching in every detail the information Fletcher had given about himself, was checked out in existing records.

Shortly after the beginning of my association with Fletcher, events propelled us into world-wide headlines. The magician Harry Weiss, known as Houdini, had been a famous performer during the 1920's and is ranked among the all-time greats of magic. After the death of his mother, to whom he was deeply attached, he attempted communication with her through mediums. This field was (and is) marred at times by fraud. Houdini, a hard man to fool, was infuriated, and embarked on a campaign of exposure of fake mediums that made headlines again and again. He had seen enough, however, to allow the possibility that not all mediums were frauds and spirit communication might be possible. Before he died (in 1926) he arranged with his wife Beatrice that whoever died first would communicate with the survivor—if communication were found possible at all—by means of a code they had used to communicate information during one of their early vaudeville acts. It was a complicated set of signals using an old popular song as key, and known only to themselves. In a case that has since become one of the classics of parapsychology, Fletcher began, in a series of sittings which commenced in February, 1928, to bring in messages purporting to be from Houdini. The news was an instant sensation in the press. Every session after the first was attended by an editor of the *Scientific American*—where the entire case was ultimately published—and taken down by a stenographer. Beatrice Houdini testified, when the long sequence was completed, that the message was the one she and her deceased husband had agreed upon, and that it had been transmitted in their private code. Fletcher and I found ourselves world-famous overnight. We were praised in the press of two continents—and denounced by skeptics from coast to coast. Not until 1967, when Fletcher and I established communication between Bishop James Pike and his discarnate son, did any demonstration of psychic reality attract such universal public attention. The Pike case will be reported in full detail—together with details not published until now—in its proper place later in this book. Our narrative has taken us, so far, to the threshold of the 1930's—a decade that opened, for me, with almost unspeakable disaster.

In 1931 I was returning from a South Carolina holiday with my younger sister Edith and a friend of hers named Grace when a speeding truck smashed into us. Edith was killed instantly, Grace died in a few hours, and I was taken to the hospital with uncertain chances of recovery. During a long convalescence a young doctor, having learned that I was supposed to have psychic abilities, began psychic experiments while I was unconscious with the morphine he had given me to relieve my pain. The doctor became so interested in these experiments that he continued the morphine dosage longer than was necessary. The result was that I came out of the hospital an unwilling addict.

Horrified at what had happened, I endured the excruciating "cold turkey" separation. Now I was free from morphine, but the withdrawal had left me a jittery nervous wreck. Weeks went by, and I could not settle down. Finally another doctor, a kindly man, suggested moderate use of alcohol. It was, to me, a novel idea—I had never indulged. Alcohol would, I discovered, cure the jitters—if taken in large enough quantities. This led to a second addiction and another urgent need for cure. I have described elsewhere the exalting spiritual experience through which I finally found relief from alcoholic addiction.[1] All that needs to be said here is that it served to underscore the difference, so often obscured in the minds of the public and its professional spiritual advisers, between psychic fact and spiritual growth.

Everyone, whether good or bad, lowly or exalted, smart or stupid, will continue after biological death to live as a personal entity capable of independent thought and action and endowed with memory—this is psychic fact. For the lack of this insight, many millions, including thousands of priests and ministers, either plod mechanically and atheistically through religious rites which no longer hold meaning for them, or abandon these rites altogether.

And everyone, whatever his level of psychic insight, must, if he is to realize his true potential as a person, labor to rise from envy, greed, fear, pride, resentment, and the other destructive emotions toward love, understanding, compassion, and the other harmonious emotions—this is spiritual growth.

Fear hinders this growth. Life cannot be lived freely and abundantly when it is in daily, even hourly fear of extinction. The greatest gift to life is removal of the fear of death: this is the conviction of the finest psychically gifted souls I have encountered in forty years of mediumship. It is the thought of the Hindu firewalkers of India; I have seen them stride unharmed through a long trench of coals so hot, after days of stoking, that ordinary people could not approach within ten feet without being scorched. It is the thought of the voodoo witch doctors of the Haitian jungles; I have been present when they have manifested overwhelming psychic force. It is the thought of the great intellectually oriented psychic researchers; I worked with Oliver Lodge and Conan Doyle when they were "on this side," and, through Fletcher, after they had "passed over." I have been "wired" with the same electronic equipment used on astronauts to learn something about space medicine. With the best of these scientists the message has always been the same: life continues after what we have been calling death.

This is very ancient knowledge, obscured today only by one of the waves of materialism that periodically engulf mankind, and through tragic misinterpretations. Theologians, with only a few exceptions, have missed the psychic wellsprings of the world's great religions. They have defined as strict prohibitions warnings originally intended as safeguards of the purity of the psychic stream.

An example is this Old Testament admonition of Leviticus: "Do not turn to mediums."

Is this a prohibition reasonable people must observe in our own time?

Let us see.

Good and Evil

2

The idea of psychic experiment produces in some people a reaction of fear, sometimes based on nothing but superstition, sometimes well-founded. It may not be out of place, therefore, to insert a word about benign and malignant psychic influences. It will be a reassuring word. In nearly half a century's experience with psychic phenomena I have never known anyone who took certain precautions to get into trouble.

"Each science," St. Clair Stobart has written, "has its own special instrument for research. The psychic faculty is for the study of spirit what the telescope is for the study of stars."[1] It makes as much sense to deny the existence of the rings of Saturn and refuse to use a telescope (as Galileo's accusers did) as to deny the dimension of spirit while refusing to exercise the psychic function.

Changing the telescope to a microscope makes the figure even more apt. Bacteriologists dealing with benign and malignant bacteria protect themselves by a technique called antisepsis. In spiritual exploration the protection is a certain attitude of mind—let us call it high-mindedness. People of good intent attract adequate psychic protection.

One does not avoid hostile psychic forces by avoiding psychic development. For several years, Leeuwenhoek was the only human being who "believed in" microbes, though these entities regularly exerted their influence, sometimes on an epidemic scale. Today's poverty of psychic understanding, combined with our century's record of spiritual and psychological disaster, sufficiently points up the parallel.

It was some time after I made the disconcerting discovery of my own psychic aptitude that I began to appreciate the full extent to which this *kind* of ability (omitting for the moment the factor of quality) had influenced man's development—explained, in fact, his essential nature. Everything really worthwhile had its origin in psychic phenomena —all the arts, most of the sciences, most of the philosophies, all the religions.

Practitioners of these higher arts have always had to deal with malignant forces. Indeed, spiritual evolution may most simply be described as the conflict between good and evil. "Know Thyself" was the motto of the Delphic Oracle. "First remove the beam from thine own eye," Jesus advised, "then you'll see more clearly to take the mote from your brother's." A famous twentieth-century society for spiritual advancement suggests a "fearless and searching moral inventory" of oneself.[2] Moses, before he could achieve full use of his very great psychic powers, endured agonizing solitary confrontation with the fact that he had taken human life.

The reason was in all cases the same—protection from evil. And, even within the restricted insights of twentieth-century psychology, it is sound. One of the greatest of spiritual dangers is the unprotected condition resulting from what psychologists call projection. The fanatical Communist blames all his troubles on the greedy capitalist, the capitalist on the impious Communist, the Nazi on the Jew, the Ku-Kluxer on the Negro, the Negro on

Whitey, while each is himself committing crimes of which he is unaware. These bring on him retaliation for which he is unprepared. How does awareness of one's own baser traits protect one? Knowing the evil in oneself equips one to recognize it elsewhere and take appropriate steps. My experience in psychic work suggests that anyone who approaches the adventure with honesty, with good will, with hope, and with some comprehension of his own limitations, will not come to harm through it.

The first recorded indication of clear psychic ability, I was fascinated to learn, dates back more than eight thousand years to around 6700 B.C. It was reassuring, at the time of my first confusion over the things that had begun happening to me, to learn that the world's religious writings, when read with even a little parapsychological insight, turned out to be mostly made up of simple records of the world's truly great mediumships.

These chronicles have two great aims—to show that human personality survives death, and to record that under certain circumstances physical materials are manipulated by nonphysical psychic forces. The method is a simple heaping up of well-attested evidence. The language, particularly in the Old Testament, is often that of a receptive but uncultivated people. But the nature of the events recorded cannot be misunderstood by anyone having even casual acquaintance with psychic events in our own time.

According to the celebrated French scholar d'Olivet, the Western religious tradition begins with the legendary barbarian priestess Voluspa, whose psychic ability brought her to prominence among the nomadic tribes of the eastern European steppes in the seventh millennium before Christ. Her first overpowering "spirit message"—or in the language of today's parapsychology, luminous apparition of a discarnate—was a plea against racial suicide. While two rival chieftains were working through the verbal preliminaries to combat, Voluspa felt "about to swoon, but still conscious" (a good description of the mental state preliminary to some psychic events). She heard her name called, looked up and saw a shining warrior who ordered her to throw herself between the two quarreling commanders (her husband and her brother), call off the intertribal slaughter they were working up to, and turn their attention to the powerful enemy that threatened both tribes. Voluspa obeyed. Her message was so charged with spirit, its outcome so successful, and her subsequent spirit messages so illuminating, that she became high priestess of a tribal religion dominated by women. These early prophetesses, d'Olivet says, delivered their messages in rhythmic sentences which provided the basis of the first formal meters of poetry.[3]

My masculine ego was not displeased to discover that men were not long in taking the psychic initiative. Women (wrote d'Olivet) found they could not always rule by truth and took to ruling by terror. On the pretext that messengers had to be sent to tribal ancestors from time to time to take them news of their descendants, Voluspa instituted human sacrifice. Nine victims a day were thus dispatched at nine-day ceremonies held every nine months. A young man named Rama—studious, thoughtful, with a bent toward religion—left the country to travel through the whole known world to learn what he could. On returning to Europe he was dismayed at the extent to which the bloody cult of human sacrifice had spread. A new cult formed around Rama's own great psychic powers—he was a healer.

This split between those who favored such "abominations" as temple harlotry and human sacrifice and those who did not accounts—I discovered—for many of the outraged fulminations of the Old Testament prophets. By the time of the great ethical and humanitarian Hebrew leaders (1800 B.C. and later) horrors in the name of religion

were so widespread in Asia Minor that the people of Israel
had to be warned against them continually. The first stern
admonitions appear in the biblical book of Leviticus. The
Lord, instructing Moses as to what the children of Israel
must be taught, says the following kinds of people shall be
put to death: those who give their children to Moloch
to be burned, those who indulge in any of a long list of
sexual irregularities, and "any man or woman who is a
medium or a wizard." This despite the facts that Moses
himself was mediumistic (he heard voices—was, in the
modern term, clairaudient—and produced automatic writing) and the whole chain of great Hebrew prophets were
highly gifted mediums!

The Old Testament range of psychic talent is overwhelming. Abraham heard voices, went into trances and
had meaningful visions. Jacob manifested discarnates physically and had conversations with them. Joseph was
strongly precognitive and could interpret dreams. Balaam
was clairvoyant and clairaudient; so was Gideon. Elisha
was precognitive. Elijah had all these powers and besides
could produce apports—the instant transport of objects to
designated and sometimes distant points.

Either it is all the most outrageous nonsense or it is a
simple, factual description of psychic phenomena. For my
own part, my direct experience allows me no choice but
to recognize it as the latter. The sitting of Saul with the
medium at Endor—a typical Old Testament transaction
—is quite modern in tone. It's the kind of thing that happens
daily with the mediums of our own time and has happened
innumerable times in my own apartment. Someone desires
a seance to communicate with a specific discarnate for a
specific reason. The medium has never met the sitter before
and at the opening of the seance knows nothing about him.
The sitting, as frequently happens, is successful: the hoped-

for discarnate comes through, the desired dialogue takes place, the sitting is ended.

As my experience in psychic matters widened, I came to understand more and more the Old Testament distaste for "mediums and wizards." God knows I am not a prude —couldn't be; my own record is too splotched with mistakes. And when we have temple harlotry and human sacrifice, it at least is not under church auspices, so we're that much improved since Old Testament times. Still, there are practicing mediums in this country, persons of quite authentic psychic ability, whom I would not recommend because they are ignorant, superstitious, morally below par, and in some cases vicious. Psychic talent, the ancients knew perfectly well, is no guarantee of moral rectitude. Distinguishing between mediums of scanty ethics and those of transcendant nobility, they called these latter "prophets." Some of the noblest people I have ever known have had psychic gifts, and some of the crookedest. At one time the best medium in England was in jail for burglary (and guilty, too)!

My inquiries into the history of the psychic gift now took a new turn. While the great Hebrews were so dramatically exploring the meditative and spiritual dimensions, that incredible development, the Greek intellect, was having comparable adventures in the stony peninsula that forms the western boundary of the Aegean Sea. The great Greek psychic was Pythagoras; his inspiration carried through Socrates, Plato, and Plotinus to Jesus and to Paul. This blending of Hebrew and Greek psychic experience gave the world Christianity, a religion which was founded on (and which departed from) history's most astounding mediumship, that of Jesus.

The name Pythagoras is known to every schoolboy through its association with the theorem describing the relationships between the squares of sides of triangles.

Pythagoras was born on the Greek island of Samos about 582 B.C. During a vision that came to him when he was a young man, he saw and sensed cosmic truths which seemed to him inexpressible by ordinary means. He tried to express them in mathematics, and this effort led to the fundamental discoveries of geometry and trigonometry. Eager for even greater insights, he went to Egypt and studied for several years under the leading Egyptian psychics. Taken prisoner during one of the wars, he was sent to Babylon, and there mastered the insights of the learned Persian psychics, the Magi. At last, after thirty-four years, he returned to Greece, his great abilities beginning to reach their prime. He revived the ancient oracle at Delphi by abolishing the decadent customs of the place and installing mediums he knew, from his studies, to be of the highest quality. He then traveled through the Greek and Roman settlements around the Mediterranean, founded institutions that in a later day would have been called churches, continuing his inquiries into the structure of the universe (he saw clearly the relationships between its material and nonmaterial aspects) and encouraging others to do so. Mathematical discoveries continued, and the harmonic principles which govern musical tones were also formulated. And mediumship reached a high level of effectiveness. The religion of Pythagoras was a powerful and elevating force for two and a half centuries.

The ministry of Jesus was the sublimest mediumship in history. Jesus was unquestionably a divinely inspired teacher and prophet on a cosmic, evolutionary mission. He was also —as another great psychic, John the Baptist, at once perceived—a medium of very great powers. Despite his own prophecy that "ye shall do even greater works," and despite the fact that phenomena similar to those he produced are occurring today, the psychic works of Jesus have not yet been equalled by any other single medium.

If one accepts, as I do, the hypothesis that Jesus was a medium, an interesting question arises. Most mediums have spirit controls. Who was the control of Jesus? Was it Abraham (he once assured an audience that he knew this patriarch)? Was it Moses or Elias (both once materialized and conversed with him in the presence of three disciples)? Or was it—as I believe—Cosmic Being itself—the Holy Spirit, God? Later theologians set him up as the "only" son of God; Jesus himself assured us we could *all* be God's sons—he made no claims to exclusiveness. To those who cared to follow the regimen he suggested, he promised to send the Spirit of Truth, who would lead through growth experience to "all truth."

Jesus emphasized again and again that psychic phenomena were never to be taken as ends in themselves, but only as illustrations of the fact that the universe is essentially spirit and not essentially matter. That he had a familiar knowledge of a spirit world that lives through eternity is often suggested, most impressively by his easy description of the discarnates Lazarus (a beggar in his earth life) and the former rich man, ending with the prophecy—which *certainly* has come true—concerning those who would not believe even if messages came "from the dead."

Jesus' recorded "miracles"—a misnomer, since these events are accomplished according to natural laws still inadequately studied—are without exception in categories regularly reported and authenticated in modern psychical research. Most striking, perhaps, are the "apports"—appearances, like the wine at Cana, the loaves at the convocation, the coin in the fish's mouth to appease the tax collector —of materials that had not been there an instant before. Numerous examples, one of them an emergence of coins from the sea quite in the New Testament manner,[4] are recorded in our own time. I have myself witnessed such events, and once found in my own hand, placed there instantaneously by a nonphysical agency, publicly and in broad daylight, a semiprecious stone. The famous episode of walking on the water is a case of levitation, a phenomenon known, as regards physical objects, to thousands of contemporary families who have experimented with table-tilting,[5] and as regards human bodies, to every serious psychical researcher.[6] Telekinesis, the movement of physical objects by nonphysical means, is one of the most common of today's psychic occurrences of the "physical" type. The rolling of the stone from the tomb of Jesus was a New Testament example. Full materializations and dematerializations (the Resurrection and later appearances of Jesus) have never been common, but have been reliably witnessed in our own time. The withering of the fig tree has been duplicated in substance, under the most rigidly supervised scientific auspices, this very year.[7] That Jesus was clairvoyant is indicated by the ease with which he took in the life situation of the woman of Samaria (clairvoyance is in our time the most widely demonstrated and most scientifically attested of the psychic gifts[8]). That Jesus was precognitive and a sensitive telepathic receiver (gifts not unusual among earth's present population[9]) is shown by his predictions of his own execution and by his instant knowledge of what his disciples were thinking. As for his healing "miracles," any modern hospital possessing a psychically oriented chaplain—and there are many—can produce medically attested records no less astonishing.

That the psychic phenomena which began in prehistory —clairvoyance, clairaudience, apports, telekinesis, telepathy, materialization, meaningful visions, discarnate communication through trance mediumship—continue in unbroken sequence to the present day is a matter of record. I have said little, in this cursory summary, of the great psychics of the East—the legendary Krishna, Lao Tsu, Buddha—or of Islam, or of Persia, or of Egypt, or of Peru, or of the primitive peoples. The testimony of all is unanimous and to the same point: there is more to the universe than can ever be known through the five physical senses, or through any instrumental extension of them.

In the Christian tradition, as in all the others, the evidence continues from where we left off: glossalalia (speaking in tongues) and astral lights (tongues of flame) —both phenomena reported in our own time—appeared as the first Christians waited for a sign at Pentecost. Peter and the other disciples developed the healing gift and precognition. Jesus appeared to Paul in spirit form and recruited him into the new religious movement. Paul, the great organizer of churches, built psychic phenomena into the very foundation stones of the Christian Church with these words in First Corinthians (12:28): "first apostles, second prophets, third teachers, then workers of miracles, then healers, helpers, administrators, speakers in various kinds of tongues."

However, once the church became a powerful worldly institution, a catastrophic change took place. The kind of psychic event that had given the church its start was now looked upon with extreme suspicion. Psychic phenomena occurring after the first few centuries A.D. were extremely suspect, if not actually regarded as works of the devil. It was risky business to display psychic ability; some gifted psychics became saints, others were burned as heretics, and it was hard to predict which way the ball would bounce. Church authorities regarded themselves as divinely appointed intermediaries between man and God. To approach God directly, or even claim that it was possible, was wicked. To have insights differing radically from those of church dignitaries could be punished by death.

A few great psychics survived all hazards and are remembered as radiant saints. The thirteenth century brought Francis of Assisi, with his levitations, ecstatic visions, and,

at the last, his stigmata. The fifteenth century produced
Joan—later St. Joan—of Arc, who was clairvoyant, clairaudient, and precognitive. Joan was telepathically receptive
and considered herself to be in communication with
spirits. Since she obtained information and controlled events
in ways that could not be accounted for by physical means,
her contemporaries took her at her word. Joan was declared
a witch, burned at the stake at the age of nineteen, and
then, some five centuries later, declared a saint. Both good
and evil psychics walked on French soil in Joan's time. One
of her contemporaries was the notorious Seigneur de Retz,
who conducted black masses, abducted and killed more than
a hundred children in human sacrifices, and was once
nearly bludgeoned to death by "poltergeist" psychic forces
propelling heavy objects.

St. Teresa of Avila, a nun, appeared in Spain in the
sixteenth century. Her psychic abilities included spirit
writing, automatic writing, clairaudience, levitation, materialization—and an exceptionally acute intelligence. Since
one of the aims of this chapter is to indicate that things
that happened long ago are also happening today, and
since levitation of the human body has always been rare, it
should be mentioned that an American psychiatrist traveling in Italy in 1960 sent back word of a monk who levitated
regularly during mass, much to the chagrin of his ecclesiastical superiors.

Lest this passage appear too heavily Catholic, let us
note that Protestants have also produced an abundance
of gifted psychics. In seventeenth-century England, George
Fox heard voices, gave himself over to the guidance of an
inner light, held meetings so packed with psychic power
that the building shook, experienced visions, and spent
a total of eight years in jail, mostly for interrupting Church
of England services and for refusing to take off his hat
when ordered to. Precognitive, Fox foresaw the Revolution

of 1688 and the Great Fire of London. He was clairvoyant, he went into trance, and he was a healer. The eighteenth century brought Emanuel Swedenborg, who spent fifty-six years becoming one of the world's acknowledged great natural scientists before giving himself over to exercising his psychic powers. Among the great psychics of all time, Swedenborg gave one of the most clearly evidential demonstrations of clairvoyance ever known. One Saturday afternoon in 1759 Swedenborg, while visiting in Gothenburg, "saw" that Stockholm, three hundred miles away, was burning. The fire spread rapidly, burned the house of a friend, and was threatening his own Stockholm residence when, about 8 p.m., it was extinguished. On Tuesday morning news of the fire reached Gothenburg from Stockholm; it had been, of course, exactly as Swedenborg described it.

Alexander Campbell (1788-1866), cofounder of the Disciples of Christ Church, railed against paying very much attention to psychic phenomena—yet he himself had psychic ability that expressed itself in visions and foreknowledge. One night in 1807 Campbell dreamed that the ship on which he and his family were sailing to America would be wrecked —he told his mother and sisters about it. The *Hibernia* was wrecked as predicted; the passengers were all taken safely to shore. During Campbell's college days he was alone in his room when a small, dark-visaged woman entered. She called his attention to what she had written on the mantle —the names of the members of his family. Then she made him understand he would go to a foreign country, be shipwrecked and rescued, would preach to large audiences, and be twice married. She then disappeared. All this came true.

John Wesley was a healer in eighteenth-century England, and more than once saw audiences carried off in transports, during which they made unintelligible sounds.

Instances of glossolalia are occurring in the United States even in 1968. In New York City, a number of seminarians went to a lecture to hear a report—a *report*, mind you, not a demonstration—of these events. Before it was over, several of them were near the trance state, struggling to keep themselves from speaking in tongues, splashing cold water on their heads to fight off the influence. The 1968 General Assembly of the United Presbyterian Church, at the behest of 150 of its ministers, authorized a comprehensive study of glossolalia as it is currently practiced throughout the country,[10] at least one new book on the subject (possibly others) has appeared within the decade.[11]

This chapter's instances have all been in the religious vein. We must now consider some psychic events of a purely secular variety.

Some Secular Prophets

3

An instance has been reported from England that illustrates in a single sequence several new and deeply significant trends in our relationships to the psychic world.[1]

A minister had undergone the shattering experience of losing a son and an only daughter within a very short time. Stunned by his double bereavement, he found all his religious education, all his ecclesiastical training, quite inadequate to restore the faith and morale necessary to carry on his day-to-day job. In the extremity of his despair he consulted a medium. From the lips of the medium he caught expressions so uniquely characteristic of his children as to convince him that they did indeed still live.

Such cases have been common in my own work. Complacent churchgoers would be shocked if they knew how many American clergymen, in their heart of hearts, are agnostics or even atheists, mechanically repeating a learned formula they no longer believe. That I have been able, with Fletcher, to help so many of those who have come to me has been one of the great satisfactions of my life as a psychic.

The clergyman under discussion some time later confided his experience to one of his parishioners, a widow. She told him the following story: "I was young when I lost my husband and at first was nearly mad with grief. I was a silly little thing without much religion and almost no faith. I had the children to raise and no one to help me." When her minister came to call he caught the full blast of her frustrated anger. "I raged against God for taking my James from me, raged at the parson for calling a God like that good." She'd have nothing to do with mediums: "Didn't believe I should get comfort that way." So she continued to scold God for not meeting her needs, letting him have it with special fury whenever she wanted to show her husband "how bonny the children were, and how clever."

At first she "felt wicked," but after a while began to feel that "God liked the honesty of it." Then one day her husband was there, "but braver and stronger and happier than I had ever known him." Did she see anything? No, "it was not a silly ghost." Or hear anything? "How could my ears hear what my eyes couldn't see?" But thereafter he appeared often enough to be a full partner in raising their children.

What had happened is obvious enough to the psychically experienced: the woman had brought into play her latent capacity for mediumship. Some projection here perhaps, the psychologist may suggest? But projection and mediumship, as we shall make clear in a later chapter, are not incompatible. What makes this case significant is that *many* people—ordinary people in ordinary occupations— are beginning to discover their psychic gifts. I encounter such cases so frequently as to be personally convinced that we are on the verge of so radical an overturn of materialistic values as to usher in an entirely new era of human experience. We are approaching a time when psychic ability will be found to be as common—and as varied in quality—as the ability to sing, or play the piano or guitar, or compose a poem or a picture. This awareness of an ultimate dimension of being may well be one of the great changes the twenty-first century will bring to man. The posture of the materialist is weakening. He is driven to more and more absurd "explanations," to more and more obvious evasions, as the psychic evidence mounts.

In ancient times psychic gifts were exercised almost entirely under religious auspices. From a quite early date, however, these phenomena also appeared in circumstances in no way connected with religion. The most famous secular psychic of antiquity was, of course, the one who warned Julius Caesar to look out for the Ides of March. He was a professional. Even more impressive work has been turned in by amateurs of our own century.

All the later work of the Irish poet W. B. Yeats was based on a remarkable sequence of psychic events that began on an October afternoon in 1917. Yeats and his bride of four days were idly passing the time of day when his wife, more or less as a lark, announced she was going to try automatic writing. The technique, generally known at the time, was simply to pass into a relaxed, receptive, drowsy mental state with a pencil and paper at hand. People endowed with this form of mediumship may begin to write unconsciously. What they write resembles, in content, the communications brought orally by mediums who work in trance. To their surprise, Mrs. Yeats turned out to have an unusually powerful psychic endowment.

"What came was so exciting, sometimes so profound," wrote Yeats, "that I persuaded her to give an hour or two a day to the unknown writer." So fascinating was the first week that he offered to give the rest of his life to piecing together the scattered messages. No, said the communicators, they had come to give him a new imagery for his poetry. Then, over a period of years, they unfolded a vast scheme embracing the entire structure and meaning of history, interpreted as a complicated fabric of two-thousand-year cycles. Three years later, Yeats had fifty notebooks full of transcriptions. He reworked these and published the whole account in a three-hundred-page book called *A Vision.* The transmission of the messages was punctuated at unexpected intervals by a wide variety of psychic displays. At one point Mrs. Yeats suddenly broke off her automatic writing and began to communicate orally, in trance. Over the years there occurred such events as loud raps, flashes of light, musical sounds, strong scents of roses or violets, apparitions of persons attired in six-teenth- and seventeenth-century clothing, and—once—a single sentence spoken in a loud voice.

One of the century's famous spirit communications, the Patience Worth series, came through another housewife and originated in the same spirit of play. Mrs. Pearl Curran of St. Louis had been given a Ouija board and occasionally spent an hour at it with a friend, seeing what they could get. For some time nothing came through but a mishmash of casual odds and ends that might easily have popped up from the subconscious of one of the people at the board. Then, on a July evening in 1913, the planchette suddenly came to life. "Many moons ago I lived," it spelled out briskly. "Again I come. Patience Worth is my name." Thus began a relationship that continued for two decades, was continuously under study by qualified experts, and became the subject of two widely read books.[2]

In point of sheer impact of personality, Patience Worth ranks with the most effective communicators ever to come through. She had wit, erudition, and literary talent. She had a sense of fun, a love of banter, a delight in conversation, and an affectionate disposition. Who she was, where she came from, and exactly when she lived remain mysteries—she found mischievous delight in keeping them so. When asked where she came from she said, "Across the sea." Once, when pressed, she revealed that she was a spinster and mentioned the date 1649 as somehow significant in her earth life. Thereafter she coyly evaded questions about her origin. "I be like to the wind, and yea, like to it do blow me ever, since time. Do ye to tether me unto today I blow me then tomorrow, and do ye tether me unto tomorrow I blow me then today."

However, complete notes were kept from the beginning, scholars went to work on her language and vocabulary, and clues were found. Her language, the items of apparel and household equipment to which she referred, were definitely English and definitely seventeenth-century or earlier. Her speech was pure Anglo-Saxon-Norman, containing almost no words of more recent origin and no references to modern vehicles, machines, utensils, or conveniences. She possessed a thorough knowledge of the flora and fauna of Renaissance England, and this she used to good effect in her poetry. Mrs. Curran, whose interests and education were musical, had no knowledge of any of these matters.

Nothing delighted Patience more than to embroil a stuffed shirt in the toils of her wit—as in this exchange:

DOCTOR: I hope Patience Worth will come. I'd like to find out what her game is.

PATIENCE: Dost, then, desire the plucking of another goose?

DOCTOR: By George, she's right there with the grease, isn't she?

PATIENCE: Enough to baste the last upon the spit. . . .

DOCTOR: She evidently thinks we're a conceited lot.

Well, I believe she'll agree you can't get far without a fair opinion of yourself.

PATIENCE: How the donkey loveth his bray!

Later, as Patience settled into her surroundings, she communicated numerous poems, some of them long and complicated, all of them competent, some having genuine literary merit. A few seem to have been composed on the spur of the moment. After transmitting this poem

Ah, wake me not!
For should my dreaming work a spell to soothe
My troubled soul, wouldst thou deny me dreams? . . .
Ah, let me dream!
The day may bring fresh sorrows
But the night will bring new dreams.

Patience, seeing that its pathos had moved Mrs. Curran nearly to tears, quickly brought a smile with this little jingle:

Patter, patter, briney drops,
On my kerchief drying:
Spatter, spatter, salty stream
Down my poor cheeks flying.
Brine enough to 'merse a ham,
Salt enough to build a dam! . . .

Mediumships are broadly classified as "mental"—cases such as those discussed up to this point in this chapter, where the central event is the communication of a message—and "physical," where events in the world of physical objects are produced by forces not acknowledged by modern materialistic science. One of the most unusual of the modern physical mediums, Daniel Dunglas Home, was also the first to be methodically studied by highly qualified scientists. Home was born in Edinburgh in 1833, brought to this country as a small child and raised in Connecticut. When he was thirteen he announced that he could work with spirits. From that time on he exercised a powerful mediumship of the physical variety. His work was widely witnessed and acclaimed. Home produced spirit writing of the kind that appeared on the wall, according to the biblical Book of Daniel, at Belshazzar's feast. At Home's seances, furniture moved (even left the floor) "by itself," ectoplasmic hands wrote messages, Home himself rose bodily into the air without visible assistance, all in the presence of expert investigators present for the sole purpose of detecting and exposing fraud. In Home's long mediumship no one was ever able to cast a shadow on the genuineness of his phenomena. One of the observers was the celebrated British scientist Sir William Crookes, mentioned later in the chapter on scientists, who must be credited with, among other accomplishments, discovery of the element thallium, and invention of the radiometer and of the fluorescent vacuum tube. At one of Home's seances, Crookes seized one of the ectoplasmic hands. "It gradually seemed to resolve itself into vapor," Crookes reported, "and faded in that manner from my grasp." Another time a hand "after hovering near me, took the pencil from my hand, rapidly wrote on a sheet of paper, threw the pencil down, then gradually faded."

"On three separate occasions," Crookes wrote, "I saw Home rise completely from the floor. Each time I had full opportunity of watching."[3] Home was always jealous of what he called his "amateur standing." Though grateful persons showered him with gifts, he never performed for pay.

Another inspired amateur in the physical field did his work during the forty-year period 1910-1950 and was repeatedly observed and extensively reported by the world-traveler, author, and Y.M.C.A. Asia Secretary, Sherwood Eddy.[4] His name was E. A. MacBeth, his home was in Rhinebeck, N.Y., and he maintained an apartment in New York City, where many of his seances were conducted. A man of independent means, he took no pay for his very extensive mediumistic work. He had been a practicing physician, had retired from medicine, and gave his time to his business affairs—and to his mediumship. Dr. MacBeth produced some of the clearest, most sustained and best witnessed "direct-voice" messages ever reported. "Direct-voice" is a technique in which, by means to be discussed in a later chapter, the voices of discarnate visitors are heard directly—that is, as coming out of the air—without utilizing the medium's vocal apparatus. He was adept in psychometry, or "object-reading," in which the medium holds a piece of personal property in his hands and receives—and relates—sometimes very extensive information about the person who possessed it. He was one of the rare mediums who could demonstrate "independent writing," distinguished from automatic writing by the circumstance that no earthside human touches pencil or paper. Mac-Beth possessed precognitive powers and—perhaps not surprising in a physician—was frequently able to effect spiritual healing. Many times, and in the presence of numerous observers, he produced the rare "apport"—the dematerialization of a distant object and its rematerialization out of the air in the seance room. Objects such as china or metal ornaments, ash trays, metal discs, taken from the homes of visitors who had come from a distance, were transported in this way.

Hardly less remarkable than MacBeth himself was his control, "Father Tobe." Tobe was, according to his own account, a doctor of philosophy from Ireland who came to the United States and died in Elizabethtown, Kentucky, in 1852. Deeply religious and immensely learned, he spotted MacBeth's psychic talent, discovered a strong personal compatibility with him, and made the doctor his instrument during the long and productive mediumship. If, as is certainly the case, people sometimes complain that spirit messages tell too little about life in other dimensions, Tobe was a notable exception. He discoursed learnedly on the subject for hours (his fascinating views are taken up in their proper place in another chapter). He had this to say about foretelling the future.

We are in eternity, not time, nor are we subject to time and its subjective conditions as you are—although our life here is dependent and has its limitations. This transcendence of time over here may help you to realize in part how persons in dreams or by clairvoyance or otherwise are able at times accurately to foresee the future by "precognition," a very frequent psychic phenomenon.

No account of distinguished mediums would be complete without mention of Edgar Cayce, whose unique career began just after the turn of the century and ended with Cayce's death in 1945, and Eileen J. Garrett, who contributed an outstanding and widely studied mediumship.[5]

Edgar Cayce was born on a western Kentucky farm in 1887, and had vivid psychic experiences, including occasional visions, from early childhood. He was intensely religious and soon gained a thorough knowledge of the Bible. In school, however, he was slow. One time when he was twelve his exasperated father drove him from early evening to nearly eleven at night to learn a spelling lesson he simply could not master. Finally, exhausted, the boy asked for a five-minute break to sleep on the book. It was granted. When he awakened he knew every word on every

page of the spelling book, letter-perfect. Despite his astounding ability to master books by simply sleeping on
them, Edgar never developed a love of learning. He quit
school at fifteen, got a copy of a wholesale stationery
catalogue, slept on it, and got a job with the firm by
demonstrating he knew their catalogue by heart. He later
earned his living as a photographer, never had much interest in money and so never had much of it.

When Cayce was twenty-one he was attacked by a
mysterious illness that caused him excruciating headaches
and loss of voice. A New York doctor treated him by
hypnosis and suggested, when he discovered his patient's
psychic talent, that Cayce might benefit from hypnotizing
himself. This Edgar did. His words while in hypnotic
sleep were recorded. They constituted the first of the more
than fifteen thousand diagnostic "readings" he did over a
period of some forty years. These, in part, were his words
on this first occasion:

> Yes, we can see the body. In the normal physical state
> this body is unable to speak due to a partial paralysis of
> the inferior muscles of the vocal cord, produced by
> nerve strain. This is a psychological condition producing
> a physical effect. It may be removed by increasing the
> circulation to the affected parts by suggestion while in
> this unconscious condition.[6]

(Note the medical manner of speaking, from the lips of a
young man who had never cracked a medical book.) In a
few minutes he said, "It's all right," and awoke—and it was.

Soon after that the devout Cayce prayed that his psychic
gifts might be used for healing, and especially for healing
children. Almost at once there was brought to him, by a
local doctor, a little girl who was having twenty convul-
sions a day and seemed in danger of losing her reason.

Cayce hypnotized himself and, while asleep, dictated instructions which the doctor followed. "In three months," reads a statement notarized and dated 1910, "she was in perfect health and is so to this day." The story of Cayce's thousands of successful diagnoses while in trance has been told many times, most notably by Thomas Sugrue in his famous book *There Is a River*. Psychical researchers are still studying the cases on file at the Association for Research and Enlightenment (Cayce Foundation) at Virginia Beach, Va.

Besides his medical work, Cayce left a prophecy, called "Earth Changes," for the remaining years of the twentieth century.[7] Strife between labor and management, a "division in our land," outbreaks of mob violence, were all predicted by Cayce before he died in 1945. There will be strife, among other places, "in the areas above Australia" (Indonesia? Vietnam?). Great land changes may be expected before 1998, with parts of coastal United States slipping into the sea, Great Lakes waters flowing into the Gulf of Mexico, portions of the lost Atlantis rising again from the ocean. Vast new temple records from antiquity will be discovered in Egypt (prophecy fulfilled in 1964). New land will arise around Bimini. "Yes, for there will be a breaking up, until the time when there are people in every land who will say that this or that shows the hand of divine interference, or that nature is taking a hand . . . let each declare whom ye will serve: a nation, a man, a state, or thy God."

Scientists Both Sides

4

It is now more than three centuries since the founding of England's Royal Society marked the beginning of modern scientific inquiry. In this time man has immeasurably increased his power to manipulate his physical environment. These new powers have brought such benefits that no responsible person is today suggesting that they be given up. Materialistic science can do so much that man tends to leap to the conclusion that it can do anything. Many honored figures in the learned community go so far as to suggest that things not explainable in orthodox materialistic terms don't really happen at all.

This presupposition, when combined with a measure of arrogance and a negative mental set, has resulted in behavior on the part of supposedly responsible scientists that at its worst has been cruel and at its best merely stupid. Let me cite an example.

I once gave a sitting for some thirty people at a midwest college noted for the quality of its scholarship and the integrity of its faculty. Careful records were kept, as usual, of what went on while I was in trance. One of the note-takers turned in the following report:

Through Arthur Ford, Fletcher gave many messages that seemed to have meaning to the people for whom they were intended. At one point he spoke of "Brazil— No, not Brazil, a country, but a name like Brazil and not a country. Anyone know what I'm talking about?" No one volunteered. Fletcher continued. "I get a name something like Brazil. Brazila. It is a person's name." Two visitors from another college spoke up; they were soon going to South America—Colombia. Fletcher didn't think this was for them. He asked whether they were going on a scholarship. They said no, and he said this had something to do with a scholarship, and with the name Brazila. No one else spoke up and after a few more attempts Fletcher dropped the subject, with obvious frustration. After the sitting one of the professors present said to another who had been present: "You know when Arthur Ford was talking about 'Brazila'? Well, I don't believe in any of this stuff so of course I refused to speak up. But I know exactly what he was talking about. The college used to have an award that was called the Brazila scholarship."[1]

Let us review what happened here. Fletcher, with his usual persistence, was continuing the work on which he has centered his being: the impressing upon mankind, by means of messages containing clearly verifiable information, that human personality, complete with powers of choice, recognition, and memory, survives after biological death. In the face of very great difficulties (some of which will be discussed presently) he brought through a highly evidential message directed to a specific person who alone would comprehend it. The message having been delivered and its content recognized, what was the response of the learned gentleman for whom it was intended? Deliberate frustration by refusal to respond. The reason? "I don't believe in any of this stuff." Is this scientific? Is it even intellectually honest? Yet this man occupies a well-paid position at a respected institution as an authority in a field where strict honesty and faithful response to signals are rigid necessities.

This kind of thing has happened so often in my experience that I am sometimes moved to ask whether the time hasn't come, after all these years of investigating mediums, when a brief investigation of academicians might also be in order. Sometimes skeptical investigators, though honest enough, are boorish to a point where only those devoted to an important cause can put up with them. In the early days of Edgar Cayce's fame an expert breezed into town from one of the prestigious New England universities, demanded full access to the Cayce premises, tumbled Edgar's meager collection of books about, branded the family and its associates ignorant simpletons. Village folks shook their heads, after his departure, and wondered who taught such people their manners.[2]

This man, though rude, was not cruel. Real viciousness has not been unknown among the more hostile investigators of psychic phenomena, imposing upon the objects of their study discomfitures and even dangers that in no way advanced the cause of comprehension. Sherwood Eddy spent a good deal of time observing the mediumship of Mrs. L. R. G. Crandon, wife of a distinguished professor of surgery at Harvard Medical School and one of the great mediums of the 1930's. Charming, educated, obliging, giving herself generously to aid in the scientific understanding of her remarkable abilities, Mrs. Crandon was more than once subject to mistreatment and even peril, particularly when she permitted researchers to handle ectoplasm. This substance is produced from the bodies of physical mediums while in trance. It disappears after a sitting and presumably is drawn back into the medium's body, of which it was originally a part. Eddy commented,

> As I recall some of the cheap tricks confessedly played on the Crandons by some of my friends, who certainly did not act as gentlemen in some of the things they did —such as covering their hands with sticky mucilage, glue or paint to place upon the ectoplasm, possibly doing bodily injury to the medium—I was compelled to admit that Dr. and Mrs. Crandon behaved much better than some of their so-called scientific investigators. I could name certain researchers who seemed to me at times to have shown a much greater witch-hunting zeal for exposing mediums who, they were convinced, were false, than they had shown for an objective, open-minded search for truth.[3]

Every responsible medium recognizes the need for objective, even skeptical inquiry into the phenomena he produces, however tiresome it may be to see successive waves of tyros labor over ground already won and argue points already proved. There are questions, scores of them, that we ourselves are in the dark about and anxious to find answers to. Conscious fraud is the least of them; the biggest problem in the deception category is the unconscious kind. The great medium Palladino, as one example, produced flawless psychic phenomena when under rigid and skeptical scientific observation, but when this was relaxed she cheated flagrantly.[4] This disturbed her; it was done while she was in trance, either by forces from outside herself or by elements of her psyche not under conscious control. Another question awaiting further study is the phenomenon, superficially resembling mediumship, called multiple personality. It has been suggested that mediums' controls are really their alternate personalities; the question of how the alternate personality gets its information is left dangling. Hypnosis theory has often been invoked. It is known that the subconscious mind under hypnosis is highly suggestible and can accomplish unusual things if they are proposed to it. Can it, if so ordered, even skip off and converse with people long dead?

Telepathy of a strictly earthbound kind—between biologically living persons—is the explanation most frequently put forth by hard-core skeptics working with mental mediums. If a given bit of information exists in any mind anywhere on earth, this theory assumes, the medium can instantly pick it out from among the infinite numbers of other bits of information similarly available and fit it precisely into the situation immediately called for in the seance. This demands feats of memory and of mind-reading far more wonderful, and revisions of conventional ideas about the structure of the universe far more drastic, than the discarnate-being hypothesis it was intended to supplant. Finally, there is evidence of auras and astral bodies that calls for still other theories in explanation (see Chap. 5). In all, there's so much to be done—enough to engage fruitfully the best minds of the species for at least a generation—so many epoch-making questions calling for reasoned and verified answers, that it's small wonder if we who are of necessity immersed in these affairs go out of our way to accommodate the serious and qualified inquirer.

I have myself worked with some distinguished researchers over a wide time-span. I knew the great Englishman Sir Oliver Lodge during the 1920's and was wired with the same electronic equipment for tracking mental and bodily processes that is used in studying U.S. astronauts in 1968. My life is, in one sense, an open laboratory file.

Perhaps the most agreeable "investigation" I ever experienced was that conducted by Sir Arthur Conan Doyle.

Doyle was a large, straightforward, hearty man of sixty-five when I met him, bursting with energy and at the height of his fame. He had studied medicine at Edinburgh and for ten years conducted a struggling practice at Southsea. Even then he was interested in psychic phenomena, and was conducting experiments in telepathy and table-tipping with a friend, a young architect. It took him twenty-five years to convince himself of the actuality of personal survival of bodily death. Meanwhile his career had been crowded with adventure and achievement. His Sherlock Holmes stories, first written on a long-shot chance to round out his meager income to meet rising family expenses, had made him famous the world over. The character Sherlock Holmes had been patterned after a real person, one of his medical professors. Doyle's psychic studies finally progressed to a point where he became one of the leading figures of the Society for Psychical Research. He served with medical units in the Boer War and in World War I, and was a member of the Olympic games committee. Tragedy had touched him in the death of his son Kingsley just before World War I.

I had been given a letter of introduction to Doyle to take along on my first trip to England. My earliest opportunity to present it came at one of Doyle's public lectures. After a brief greeting he invited me to sit on the platform during his talk. Doyle was a fine lecturer and I a rapt listener. At the end of the lecture Doyle, to my complete consternation, turned to his audience and, after acknowledging its applause, said, "A well-known American medium, Arthur Ford, is with us tonight. I am going to ask him if he will now give a public demonstration of his clairvoyant gift." I staggered to my feet. I had never made any claim to being a professional medium. Up to then I had considered my platform appearances to be only tentative experiments. Soon my nervousness passed; I felt open on the spirit world. Messages for members of the audience poured in, sometimes bringing sobs of recognition or gasps at revelation of things it would have been impossible for me to know by ordinary means. The following day, the London *Express* carried a story of the event under Doyle's by-line: "One of the most amazing things I have seen in forty-one years of psychic experience was the demonstration by Arthur Ford." He had checked the accuracy of Fletcher's messages with members of the audience and we had "passed"! Thereafter, my visits with the gallant Sir Arthur, and my sittings with his family and friends, were highlights of my trips to England as long as he lived.

Among the psychical researchers I have known, easily the most distinguished, in point of scientific honors heaped upon him, was Sir Oliver Lodge. One of the world's foremost physicists, Lodge had been president of four learned scientific societies besides the Society for Psychical Research. A man in his vigorous seventies when I knew him (he lived to be ninety), he was courteous and considerate while at the same time capable of devastating satire when need arose—he once indignantly suggested the SPR had become a society for the imputation of fraud. His lifelong passion was the reconciliation of science and religion. As a physical scientist he had had few peers. He made pioneer contributions in radio, X-ray technology, and electronic theory, was head of one of the great English universities (Birmingham), and for all this had been knighted. Like Conan Doyle, Lodge had lost a son (Raymond, who was killed in World War I), had been convinced of survival before this tragedy, and had communicated with his dead son through mediums. These dialogues were published in Sir Oliver's book *Raymond* in 1916. His other books on psychic matters include *The Survival of Man* (1909) and *Reason and Belief* (1911). One of the greatest of researchers, he was well able to be thorough without being rude or inconsiderate. Lodge's technique during the stay at his home of the famous Bostonian Mrs. Piper, the one great medium who was never accused of fraud, is thus described in his own words:

> Mrs. Piper's correspondence was small, something like three letters a week, even when the children were away from her. The outsides of her letters nearly always passed through my hands, and often the insides, too, by her permission. . . . I obtained permission and immediately personally overhauled the whole of her luggage. Directories, biographies . . . and the like were entirely absent. In fact there were scarcely any books at all. The eldest child at home was aged nine, and the amount of information at his disposal was fairly well known to us. My wife was skeptically inclined and guarded in her utterances. . . . Strange sitters frequently arrived at 11 A.M., and I admitted them myself straight into the room where we were going to sit; they were shortly afterwards introduced to Mrs. Piper under some assumed name. The whole attitude of Mrs. Piper was natural, uninquisitive, ladylike and straightforward. If anything was noticeable it was a trace of languor and self-absorption, very natural under the trying condition of two long trances a day. . . .[5]

Each of the important names of early scientific psychical research—F. W. H. Myers, Henry Sidgwick, Edmund Gurney, W. J. Crawford, William James, Sir William Crookes, Doyle, Lodge, J. B. Rhine—represents a contribution that has endured. Together they cemented psychical research to the body of modern science in a way that can never again permit complete separation, much as extreme materialists may try.

The poet and essayist Myers, the Cambridge philoso-

pher Sidgwick, and the psychologist Gurney, founders of
the Society for Psychical Research, gave the movement
sanity, organization, and clear purpose. "The aim of the
Society," said its first (1882) announcement, "will be to
approach these various problems without prejudice or
prepossession of any kind, and in the same spirit of exact
and unimpassioned inquiry which has enabled Science to
solve so many problems, once not less obscure nor less
hotly debated."

Myers followed through by producing his classical six-
hundred-page study, still unfinished at his death in 1901,
called *Human Personality and Its Survival of Bodily Death*,
a universally acknowledged landmark. W. J. Crawford,
physics professor at Belfast University, greatly advanced our
understanding of physical phenomena by weighing and
photographing mediums during seance, revealing the struc-
tures of the mechanisms, built of ectoplasm from the medium's body, by which objects were moved. William James,
the philosopher, psychologist, and Harvard Medical School
professor described by *Columbia Encyclopedia* as "the
most influential American thinker of his day," contributed
tremendously with his discovery of Mrs. Piper's mediumship, his careful studies of it and conclusions about it,
and his encouragement of other scholars to carry on where
he had left off. The Oxford sage Sir William Crookes (dis-
coverer of the element thallium, inventor of the fluorescent
tube and the radiometer, pioneer in electronics) contributed his great studies of the peerless physical medium
D. D. Home, and also did much valuable work to establish
what mediumistic effects could be faked and what could
not. Doyle and Lodge donated their geniality, their prestige, their integrity, and their exceptional energy in a variety of important ways. Duke University's Professor J. B.
Rhine developed techniques of value in laboratory testing
for certain limited but important indices of psychic ability.

Some of these great pioneers continued their contributions after biological death. By the end of 1901 all three founders of SPR—Myers, Sidgwick, and Gurney—were dead. Shortly thereafter began the "Cross-Correspondences," the most elaborate fabric ever transmitted mediumistically as a coherent and identifiable single unit. The whole communication took thirty years to transmit and filled two thousand pages of transcribed automatic writing. These messages and comments on them fill three thousand pages of the SPR *Proceedings* between 1906 and 1938. They were sent by the three SPR founders and four associated discarnates and received—in separate fragments, so that no message made sense until matched with the others in the same sequence—by five separate mediums, each working independently. The messages were designed on the "other side" to settle once and for all the thorny question of whether mediumistic communications might possibly be "lifted" telepathically from the minds of persons biologically living. For these messages, this possibility was ruled out.

The method was to contrive messages in literary symbols so extremely esoteric as to be known only to a very few living persons—scholars of most finely-drawn literary and historical specialization—but known to none of the mediums selected as receivers. Connections were then shown between the messages and their senders (they were signed "Myers" or "Gurney" or sometimes just initialed), establishing an overwhelming probability that the messages could have originated nowhere but with the signers. Circumstances were created so that no single medium could possibly have conceived the whole design as finally revealed. The entire effort has woven into it the revelation of a plan for ultimate world peace—after several wars of adjustment—based on a more humane order of things and promoted by a great assemblage of discarnates of which the cross-correspondents are members and prophets.

Conan Doyle, who died in July, 1930, contributed suggestions, through my mediumship, to his own authorized biography. He was again heard from, under dramatic circumstances, in October of the same year. Arrangements for a seance with Eileen Garrett had been made by Harry Price, of the research laboratory. The main purpose of the sitting was to get in communication with Doyle. Doyle came through, and strongly, but not until after an event Price later described as "the most remarkable I have known throughout my experience of psychic matters."

The session began about 3 P.M. in full daylight. The sitters took their places at a table in front of the medium, who occupied an armchair. She closed her eyes and yawned, then relaxed to the point of nearly sliding off the chair. In about five minutes she was completely in trance. Immediately her control, called Uvani and using heavily accented English, began to speak: "It is Uvani. I give you greetings, friends. Peace be with you in your life and in your household. I see for the moment I-R-V-I-N-G or I-R-W-I-N. He says he must do something about it. He is not coming to you—does not belong to anyone—apologizes for coming, for interfering. Seems to be anxious to speak to a lady in the body. Speaks of Dora, Dorothy, Gladys. He says: 'Never mind about me, but do, for heaven's sake, give this to them. The whole bulk of the dirigible was entirely and absolutely too much for her engine capacity.'"

The voice of the medium then changed, and a new personality announced himself as Flight-Lieutenant H. Carmichael Irwin, captain of the dirigible R-101. This craft, a British lighter-than-air ship had crashed near Beauvais in France early in the morning of October fifth. Irwin, speaking through the medium, seemed very excited. In a long discourse—rapid speech interrupted by pauses—he gave a specific and very technical account of the R-101's troubles:

> Engines too heavy . . . elevator jammed. Explosion
> caused by friction in electrical storm. Flying too low
> altitude and could never rise. Disposable lift could not
> be utilized. Load too great for long flight. Same with
> SL-8—tell Eckener. Cruising speed bad and ship badly
> swinging. Severe tension on the fabric, which is chafing.
> Starboard strakes have started . . . Too short trials
> . . . Airscrews too small. Fuel injection bad and air
> pump failed . . . Fabric all waterlogged and ship's nose
> is down. Impossible to rise. Cannot trim. You will
> understand that I had to tell you. There were five occa-
> sions I had had distinct trouble—new type of feed abso-
> lutely and entirely wrong. Two hours tried to rise but
> elevator jammed. Almost scraped the roofs of Achy.
> Kept to railway . . . From beginning of trouble I knew
> we had not a chance, knew it to be the feed, and we
> could never rise. I am anxious about the health of a
> lady and child—am very worried over everything private.

Price's notes continue: "Medium's voice changes, Uvani
now speaks: 'He does not come to us.' He says: 'Bore,
capacity, feed and gas. We could never rise.' (Medium
relapses into silence and after a pause, Uvani speaks again
and 'Irwin' entity appears to have gone.)" None of the
sitters at this seance had any technical knowledge of airships or their engines; the medium had never owned a car
or any kind of engine and knew nothing about aeronautics
or engineering. A transcript of the sitting was made and
sent to various authorities, including the British Air Minister, Sir John Simon, who had been appointed to con-
duct a public investigation of the disaster (which had occurred only fifty-five hours before the sitting), and an officer who had participated in the building of the R-101. The

last-named, a highly qualified aircraft technician, certified
the Irwin communication to be technically correct in a
line-by-line analysis:

Dirigible too much for engine capacity. *Agrees with popular opinion.* Useful lift too small. *Obvious from ballast discharged.* Elevator jammed. *Thought probable by many informed opinions.* Same with SL-8—tell Eckener. *SL-8 has been verified as the number of a German airship, SL standing for Schutte Lanz. This verified only after going through complete records of German airships (i.e., it was not known to technical expert beforehand) but would have been known to Irwin. Dr. Eckener was a builder of dirigibles. . . .* Engines wrong. *In accordance with facts.* Too short trials. *Admitted.* Airscrews too small. *Believed correct by informed opinions.* Almost scraped the roof of Achy. *Achy is not shown on ordinary maps but is shown on large-scale flying maps such as Irwin had. It is a village north of Beauvais on R-101's route.* Kept to railway. *Correct. . . .*[6]

Psychical research in recent years has taken a new turn
that holds most exciting promise—the study of the aura
and of the astral body. One of the pioneers in this new field
is a Turkish-born American woman doctor, Shafica Karagulla. Dr. Karagulla earned her M.D. at the American University in Beirut. After completing her qualifications in
psychiatry at Edinburgh and making some notable contributions in the field of electric shock therapy, she became
a member of the Royal College of Physicians (Edinburgh),
Britain's highest medical qualification. In 1952 she moved
to Canada to serve as a psychiatric consultant on the staff
of the world-renowned brain surgeon, Dr. Wilder Penfield.
    While in Canada, Dr. Karagulla was given a book on the
work of Edgar Cayce. The book, she writes, "shattered all

my hard-won theories about the nature of man's mind."[7]
At about this time a teaching appointment to the faculty
of the Downtown Medical Center, State University of
New York, brought her to the United States, and she became an American citizen. Still puzzling over the Cayce
phenomena, she went to Virginia Beach to study the Cayce
records firsthand. The result: psychical research became
her "life project."

As persistent inquiries gradually widened her acquaintance among psychically gifted people, Dr. Karagulla made
an astonishing discovery: most of them kept their psychic
talents a secret. She discovered a woman Ph.D. and corporation executive with a gift for psychic diagnosis almost
rivaling Cayce's. Two physicians were outstanding psychic
diagnosticians, another was a psychic healer, a mathematics
professor could memorize whole books at a glance, a surgeon
knew precognitively which operations would be successful. All, through using their psychic gifts constantly, kept
knowledge of these talents from their associates, who would,
they knew, misunderstand and misinterpret. Nevertheless,
an insurance accountant could tell by psychometry—object-reading—how long the author of a signature placed in
his hands could be expected to live. The psychic ability of
an army officer to assess character led to the detection of a
foreign spy in a key government position. "Perhaps," Dr.
Karagulla wrote in 1967, "the human mind is developing
a perceptive faculty that can quickly encompass the world
of facts and move directly to perceive meaning and relationships."

The most effective of the psychic diagnosticians so far
studied by Dr. Karagulla did her work by utilizing her
ability to see clearly the astral body—the indestructible
second body of radiant energy that accompanies and inter-
acts with every flesh-and-blood body—and point out its
abnormalities. Because of the growing recognition of this

vital aspect of human personality, and because my own experience has confronted me countless times with irrefutable evidence of its existence, I devote the next chapter to a discussion of the second body—this "astral" body—of man.

The Two Bodies of Man

5

One of man's oldest assertions concerning his own basic nature, stated in prehistory and verified by the psychically informed of our own day, is that he has *two* highly energized bodies. One is of tissue, bone, and blood, the other of pure psychic energy. Sometimes the second or spirit body is seen objectively by independent observers. The case of the Vietnam veterans mentioned in the first chapter of this book is an example. There have been many other instances over the years.

Back in the days of sailing ships, the schooner *Julia Hallock*, commanded by Captain J. S. Clarke, was once off the Grand Banks and westbound. The first mate, Robert Bruce, came into the captain's cabin to calculate his noon observation of the sun. When he'd finished his absorbed figuring he announced the ship's estimated position. Meanwhile, unnoticed by Bruce, the captain had left the cabin. Bruce, getting no response to his announcement, looked at the captain's chair. There, looking silently at him with a fixed stare, sat a total stranger. Bruce ran to the deck, found the captain, and returned to the cabin. The stranger was gone, and a thorough search of the ship did not turn him up. On the captain's slate, however, was written, "Steer to the nor'west." Clarke ordered the ship to be put on this course. About three in the afternoon they came upon a bark which had for many days been frozen fast in the ice. Its passengers and crew were in desperate straits. On board was the man Bruce had seen three hours earlier in the captain's cabin of the *Julia Hallock*. Questioned, the man said he had fallen asleep about noon. He did not recall dreaming. When taken about the *Julia Hallock* he said the ship seemed familiar, though he did not recall ever having been on her. He was given the captain's slate and, without being shown the reverse side, asked to write "Steer to the nor'-west." The slate was then turned over to reveal the first message; the handwriting was the same on both sides.[1]

This projection of the spirit body—being seen at two places at the same time—has been observed in every era from the famous Greek mystic Pythagoras in the sixth century B.C. to Padre Pio, the great Italian psychic of our own day. Psychically sensitive doctors and nurses sometimes see such "doubles" in modern hospitals at moments of death.

More commonly, knowledge of the second body derives from direct subjective experience. Is there a family in the land without some member, in injury, coma, or serious illness, who has not stood at death's threshold—and come back to report a dimension, beyond the world of the five senses, where one is still very much alive? I know of a man, young at the time (now a member of Congress) desperately ill and in coma, whose mother formed a prayer group and prayed for his recovery. He got well—and made his mother promise never to do such a thing again. The land he had seen in spirit, he said, was far more splendid than the one he returned to!

Every war produces out-of-body experiences. C. K.

Jenkins, then a British soldier, was hit during the fighting at Ypres in 1917. "My body," he later related, "was blasted from me so quickly I was not aware of its falling. I went on without it, feeling vitally alive and free. Then I realized I'd have to go back." After his recovery he said the experience made him realize "my body is not really me, but only a cloak or skin I wear."

Sam Bourne, a London fireman, was in the fire station when it received a direct hit during the air raids of World War II. "I heard a roar," he said, "and then was out of my body. I could see the earth-body lying under a joist. I was about five feet above it, free as air and feeling no pain. I was conscious of every detail in the room, and I had a form. A friend had been sitting by the window, and I thought, 'I must go and help her.' Then, with what I can only describe as a thunderclap, I was back in my body and we were being rescued by soldiers. I will never forget the glorious feeling of freedom and lightness while I was functioning in my spiritual body. If this is 'death,' why worry?"[2]

A kind of luminous silver cord, connecting the physical with the spirit body, is often reported in association with these experiences. The understanding usually reported is that if this cord were severed it would be impossible to return to the flesh-and-blood state. A native of Australia, Mrs. E. Herrick, found herself out of the body and passing through a closed door. She tried, but failed, to move an electric light switch. Looking back she saw, trailing behind her, "a long cord or streamer of light" connecting her with her physical body. The experience brought what she considered "utterly incontrovertible proof" of survival.[3]

One of the most vividly real experiences of my own life was just such an out-of-body excursion. It forever lifted the problem of survival—for me—out of the realm of faith and brought it clearly down to the plane of realism. All the objective evidence of survival I had accumulated in thirty years—I had traveled round the world and had sittings with the great mediums of our day—became by comparison unimportant. I was critically ill. The doctors said I could not live, but as good doctors will, they kept fighting. I was in the hospital at Coral Gables, not expected to last the night. I heard a doctor speak to a nurse: "He might as well be comfortable, give him the needle." I wondered how long it would take to die. Then I was floating in the air over my bed. I saw my body, but took no more interest in it than in a castoff coat. Then total, timeless unconsciousness. I awoke from this floating through space, with no sense of having a body as I had known my body. Yet it was I, *myself*. I was in a green valley with mountains on every side, and everywhere an indescribable brilliance of light and color. Coming toward me from all sides were people I had known and thought of as dead. Those who had passed on in old age were young, those who had passed over as children were in mature spirit bodies. I was shown all the things they seemed to think I should see. Many times I have journeyed to foreign countries, been met by friends and introduced to the customs of the country, and taken to various points of interest. It was like that. I missed a number of people I had expected to see, and asked about them. Immediately the light grew dim, colors faded. Through a haze I saw those I had asked for; my body became heavy; earthly thoughts crowded into my mind; I knew I was in a lower sphere. I cried out to them and they seemed to hear me, but I could not hear their reply. Then a gentle, radiant person stood by me and I was restored. Everyone was happily intent upon mysterious errands. Some I had known well took no interest in me, while others I had known but slightly seemed attracted—the law of affinity determined relationships here. At one point a court of higher beings considered my condition. The Bible speaks of angels and archangels—could these spirits have belonged to that order? They had little interest in the usual misdemeanors so frowned upon in earth society, but were seriously concerned about waste of valuable energy, dissipation of opportunity to accomplish what I knew I was meant to fulfill. It was made clear I would have to go back. At the doorway of return I balked like a spoiled child in tantrum—braced my feet and fought against going. There was a sudden sense of hurtling through space, and I found myself looking into the face of a nurse—in Coral Gables. I had been in coma, almost lifeless, for two weeks.

Spiritual journeys of this kind have been made by people, sick and well, ever since there were people. "I know a man," wrote St. Paul, one of history's great sophisticates in psychic matters, "who fourteen years ago was caught up into the third heaven[4] . . . there are celestial bodies and terrestrial bodies . . . it is sown a physical body and raised a spiritual body."[5] Twentieth-century psychology has never succeeded in "analyzing away" these experiences, or reducing them to the level of ordinary dreams. Out-of-body experiences routinely have certainly features which do not routinely occur in dreams. There is the beginning reality of floating in an actual place—not a dream-place—and seeing, in detail, actual objects, including one's own physical body. There is the frequent mention of a luminous cord connecting body and spirit, and the feeling ("or e'er the silver cord be loosed"—Ecclesiastes) that if this cord were to be severed the two bodies would be permanently parted and the physical body would die. These and other circumstances "are inexplicable"—wrote psychologist Robert Crookall in 1965—"except on the hypothesis of an objective 'astral' or 'soul' body. Though some of the doubles people claim to have seen are doubtless hallucinations, many were, practically certainly, real."[6]

Since we on this earth are—right now—spirits as well as

bodies, observations of the second body do not always wait upon a death's-door experience. Many psychical researchers are convinced that the "aura" so often observed —and sometimes even registered on instruments—is an emanation of the second or spiritual body, which in normal, healthy earth-life interpenetrates and coincides with the physical body. Edgar Cayce, psychically the most gifted person I have ever known, could make his medical diagnoses very accurately by directly observing the patient's aura. Clairvoyants who see the aura feel they are seeing it with their ordinary eyesight. "I *see* it, that's all; it's *there.*" The gift in some degree must be fairly common; I can name offhand some thirty people who have it. From this display of light, color, and energy they can read a patient's physical and emotional health. Though it is not a specialty of mine, I, too, can see the aura if I try. A serious effort is being made by a scientist formerly with RCA to define the limits of the aura by instrument. Sensitives of many centuries and cultures have associated particular aural colors with particular conditions. White around the head, for example, is taken to indicate a highly developed spiritual nature—hence the halos medieval artists painted around the heads of saints.

Because her superb medical and psychiatric training enable her readily to separate symptoms of abnormal psychology from genuine psychic phenomena, the newly published (1967) findings of Dr. Shafica Karagulla have a special value.[7] Dr. Karagulla's most productive aura-reader, a businesswoman given the pseudonym "Diane," sees the aura in unusual detail. Its elements react visibly (to her!) with the parts of the physical body, with special flurries of aural activity around the important organs, nerve centers and glands. She once diagnosed an intestinal blockage until then unknown either to patient or physician. Within seventy-two hours the aural diagnosis was confirmed by

X-ray and the stoppage remedied by surgery. On another occasion Diane predicted the onset of a serious condition (Parkinson's disease) a year and a half in advance. It was not, she said, done by precognition, but by recognition of activity in the aural structure that would in due course bring disaster upon the physical organism. Three or four hours is required by this sensitive for a complete reading. Diane can read the doctor as clearly as the patients, and once told her she was thoroughly annoyed with a certain patient—true, but, the doctor thought, well concealed. Asked how she knew, Diane reported "little red spots, like measles," in the doctor's emotional field. This area, she says, extends a foot or so from the body in a large oval. A more compact energy body interpenetrates the physical body and, as seen by Diane, extends an inch or so beyond the skin as a close replica.

That the human body gives off radiation has been known scientifically since 1923, when it was measured by the Leningrad scientist Alexander Gurwitsch. George W. Crile demonstrated in 1934 that brain tissue gives off radiation in the visible, infra-red, and ultra-violet ranges. The strongest human radiations—reported the Cornell researcher Dr. Otto Rahn—emanate from the fingertips of the right hand, a fact long known to psychical healers. Some sensitives radiate to such a degree that they cannot be employed in any enterprise involving undeveloped photographic film; their touch or even near approach "exposes" it. This effect suggests a new possibility—will refinements in photographic techniques some day bring us even more specific knowledge of man's second body and its aura?

The physicist-engineer turned psychical researcher G. N. M. Tyrrell, a leader of world thought in psychic matters until his death in 1952, has restated, in terms of twentieth-century science, St. Paul's classical postulate of man's two bodies. Tyrrell felt that the physical and spirit bodies belonged, from the very beginning, in two distinctly separate categories of existence.

> The material organism [Tyrrell wrote] is the aspect of something belonging first and last to the finite level we now occupy, while the real human being—the personality—is by nature a stranger to that level. The strictly physical body is no more to be identified with the person when it is alive than when it is dead. . . . Our physical universe is not unique in the scheme of things. If, when we see it, we are indeed looking at the house of reality, then we are looking at one façade of that house only. Matter is not the despotic sovereign for which we have mistaken it; the brain is not the physical correlative of consciousness, but merely a link connecting the personality with the finite level. The body left behind at death never was part of the person who used it. It was an aspect of something which essentially belongs to the finite level of our present world and which therefore remains on it—something that was only borrowed by the inhabiting personality and used by it as a temporary vehicle of expression. Before the death stage the stretching of the personality has long been "loosening the silver cord."[8]

It has been necessary to review this ground, to establish that man has a spiritual body—his really important one—as well as a physical body, before we can go on to any discussion that makes sense of what really happens in an actual seance.

What Actually Happens
in a Seance?

6

When the consequences of acknowledging what happens at an ordinary seance, of the kind I have now given at least eight thousand times, are fully understood, they are seen to be quite breath-taking.

Examples abound. The simple admission of facts now established as irrefutable (my work has been closely studied by some of the ablest scientific minds of two generations) would mean an abrupt end of materialistic causality in science and positivism in philosophy. Psychological theory would have to be reconstructed to give a central position to spiritual values and entities not at present acknowledged at all.

Physiology would have to be rewritten, if the work of the physical mediums were also to be taken into account, to allow for a substance that emanates from the human body, is translucent, and is able to exert measurable force on physical objects at the direction of a mind in hypnotic trance. Religious assertions habitually set aside by many as irrelevant would have to be seriously reassessed. The personal life of each individual would have to be replanned to allow for a life span extending beyond biological death and perhaps into eternity. Lawyers and sociologists would similarly have to take into consideration social values appropriate to a human existence indefinitely prolonged.

It is little wonder, when one thinks on it, that so many specialists trained in established disciplines hastily change the subject when questioned about psychic phenomena. Merely raising the issue may place hard-won vested positions in jeopardy. It is easier, up to a point, to evade the issue than to broaden one's thinking to include new and relevant fact. I have noticed that those specialists who most vociferously deny psychic phenomena are those who have never troubled much to face up to the evidence. Reform never comes easily. Sometimes I feel something very like compassion while watching a truly learned man struggle with the issues my work is bound to raise. It is a wrenching, sometimes agonizing thing to part with preconceptions brainwashed into us from birth. "The world is full of specialists," wrote Tyrrell, "who take their subjects too literally because they believe their knowledge to be final. Each working in his own groove, he is oblivious to all the others, and regards his own subject as providing the key to the universe. One man will base his life's work on beliefs another will regard as not worth five minutes' consideration. But the two never meet to have the matter out."[1]

Physical and psychic researchers do have common ground in one pervasive truth: the world of the five senses is a world of illusion. The most solid-looking brick is mostly empty space. The reality of human existence has dimensions unseeable with the physical eye. We who explore the psychic realm are saved from at least one of the traps that beset truth-seekers: dogmatism. We know only that we stand on the rim of a limitless dimension, governed by natural law and now opening up for man to explore. Beyond that, observed facts must be organized by simple conjecture and hypothesis.

In scientific tradition, the favored hypothesis is the one which provides the simplest and most plausible explanation of observed facts. In the case of the phenomena of trance mediumship, the two-bodies-of-man hypothesis most directly explains what is seen actually to happen. By this theory, both bodies are born together and grow together until the material body dies. The spirit body is by this time able to exist on its own and continues its career, complete with energy, purpose, and memory, in the society of similar real though immaterial entities. Any other theory—and there have been some ingenious ones based on telepathy, thought-transference, and projection—calls for marvels of human resource so extreme as to stretch credulity almost past the breaking point. So, until a more explicit postulate comes along, we stick with the simplest theory. The nature of the society the spirit-body joins is still a guess, though there have been some interesting clues.

What happens superficially at a seance is prosaic enough. A medium appears to be talking in his sleep in a reclining chair. Actually, by means well understood and described in conventional medical literature, he has placed himself in hypnotic trance (sometimes mediums-in-training are put to sleep by hypnotists until they master the knack themselves). From one to thirty people—the "sitters"—are seated around him. Now and then, when addressed by the medium's voice, one of the sitters speaks. A tape recorder takes down the proceedings. The average seance lasts about an hour.

The communications system in operation in this quiet scene is amazingly complex. By the two-bodies theory, each communication involves at least four people: the discarnate originator of the message, the discarnate control, the medium, and the sitter.

That this arrangement has certain built-in difficulties is obvious from what we know about communications between normal incarnate people. How often does it happen that two people living in the same dwelling, or two branches of the same family, are "not speaking"—communications that could take place never do, because of lack of desire or positive aversion. In the classroom, some pupils on some days are excited about the subject matter and recite enthusiastically; at other times the teacher complains that they cannot be "reached"—talked with. The difficulty of one generation communicating clearly with another is well known, and the "in-law problem"—minor cultural differences between families of the same national heritage—often renders communications stilted or impossible. Dialog with people from whom we have been separated for a number of years is sometimes strained. Suppose a quiet party were being given by people you never knew very well and didn't particularly like, at which the conversation was centered on things that interest you not in the least. Would you go? All these obstacles and many more are present when we attempt communication with discarnates. They are people, and behave like people.

"We have our own version of the telephone," Fletcher once reported. Word somehow gets around to discarnates who may be interested in the sitters at a given seance that the occasion is pending. Usually attendance is governed by what F. W. H. Myers called "the law of love and friendship and common interest." Close relatives and friends who have crossed over, persons once involved in parallel lines of work (whether they knew any of the sitters or not) are likely to heed the call. Sometimes so many show up that a master of ceremonies is required to maintain order, see that people take turns, and make sure that no single discarnate monopolizes the conversation. This is one of the ways in which the services of a control—in my own case the estimable Fletcher—are invaluable. The control takes over the bodily mechanism hospitably vacated for the occasion by the sleeping medium. The hypnotic sleep, incidentally, is very deep; pins have been stuck into my flesh during trance without my waking. From this new position (according to one version of the situation) the control accepts messages from waiting discarnates and relays them through the medium's physical body to the sitters. Messages between discarnates are transmitted not only as words but sometimes as thought-symbols: "Big Ben . . . a watch . . . a clock . . . oh yes, he's saying it's just a matter of time."

The above, as I have said, is one conception of the mechanics of trance. There is another version, made available to us in a most unusual way. Some years ago I had a sitter, a woman, who was most persistent in questioning every discarnate she talked with on exactly these points—what was it like on the other side?—exactly how were messages transmitted? Finally, one day, her persistence brought results. A discarnate who identified herself as Ruth Finley came in—the "Joan" of the Darby-and-Joan sequence and a collaborator with Stewart Edward White in the famous description of the afterlife, as given from discarnate sources, called *The Unobstructed Universe*. Joan came prepared, this time, with an account of relations within the "unobstructed universe"—world of discarnates —and of transactions between that world and our own.

"Joan" reaffirmed the basic observations of the aura-readers: that all existence is energy in some form, that the higher or mental energy survives death, the lower or physical does not. However, she attached a new significance to these facts where trance communication was concerned. Because there is a degree of interplay of mental energy and physical energy in every cell, no physical body can safely be left mind-free for very long. In trance, another personality of about the same energy-pattern—the control—moves in, as it were, to keep store. Thus Fletcher is, in a limited way, "alive" for the time being, while I have the experience of being "dead"—free to roam, for a while, in the unobstructed universe.

It was a new idea to me. I had always thought of myself as simply "out" while in trance; I brought back no memories of fresh experience. There are still things about this concept that puzzle me. At the same time there are points that Joan's explanation clears up—in particular, those passages in transcripts of sittings which are pretty obviously simply me spouting my own ideas. Joan explained it this way: "Sometimes Ford gets so interested in what's being said over here that he wanders off with his cronies and lets somebody else man the station." Or, if the subject matter of the seance is of special interest to me, I seem likely to horn in and speak my piece!

I suppose every conscientious workman has that bit of the perfectionist in him that prevents him from ever being wholly satisfied with his work. Certainly this is true of the topflight mediums I have known. We are far more painfully aware of our shortcomings than any of our critics could possibly be—we know the difficulties firsthand. Halting, broken messages, clumsily phrased, wooden, without the flair of the personality of the source communicator—these things are the mark of the tyro, but they are almost inevitable while the new medium is learning his trade. Imagine, if you can, moving into an entirely strange body (as control) and trying, even in a limited way, to operate it. Wouldn't it take you a while to learn where the gadgets were? Or, on the earth side, imagine vacating your own body and turning it over to be inhabited for a time by somebody else. A certain amount of mutual accommodation is involved, a certain protocol. This has to be learned.

A common criticism—that communications involving

special knowledge lack fulsome detail—I find quite unfair. Any communication relayed by Fletcher and me is passed through our minds, and cannot transcend our own stock of memories, information, and vocabulary. Fletcher has a fine native intelligence, a ready wit, and, considering his opportunities, is astonishingly well informed. On my part, I try in a general way to keep up with things. But no one can know everything about every specialty. It is not unusual for us to deal in a single seance with people of such disparate interests as a professor of English, a nuclear physicist, a state governor, and a television announcer. Could Fletcher and I—or anyone else for that matter—possibly deal at the expert's level with all these specialties?

Could Einstein impart his newest mathematical insights to a football star? Or Mozart report on the universal music to a neighborhood grocer? Or Rembrandt discourse on art to a teamster? Even in the physical body and on the solid ground of earth, do the chemist and the choreographer ever really spark? The solution, of course, is for the specialists to develop mediumship, which they perfectly well could do if they made the effort. It might even be worth it, in terms of rewards to humanity. What might physical science gain from an hour with Albert Einstein, or the ballet from an interview with Pavlova, or symphonic music from a session with Toscanini—if transmitted by mediums who understood the language and subtleties of their specialties?

Some critics have complained that, when one considers the vast possibilities of communicating from the world beyond, many of the discarnate communications seem trivial. These trivia, however, in my mediumship, run to a special pattern, and are so important I devote a special chapter to them a little farther on. A quite different kind of trivia, taking the form of foolishness or even spite, have in some mediumships caused considerable static. The discarnates with whom W. B. Yeats and his wife were in touch gave such entities the name "frustrators." Once, when told not to take anything down because a summary was forthcoming, the instruction turned out to be pure mischief. "From such and such a day, such and such an hour," Yeats was then told, "all is frustration"—indicating the loss of several days' work in getting through the full and correct message.

Frustrators on the flesh-and-blood level, my experience suggests, cause more obstruction than anything originating beyond. Stiff, suspicious, uncommunicative people are no fun in any sphere. When the invitations go out, who would want to go to *that* kind of a party? Best results are obtained with lively, interested, responsive, question-asking sitters. When you go to a seance be prepared to meet almost anyone and pass the time with him pleasantly and chattily. If you have questions, ask them; it adds to the occasion.

Some communicators come through with almost explosive force, full of almost desperate urgency. The R-101 commander already mentioned was one such case. The now famous case of James Pike, Jr., twenty-two-year-old son of Bishop James A. Pike, was another. Young Pike shot himself to death in a New York City hotel room in February, 1966. About two weeks later, physical phenomena of psychic origin began to occur in Bishop Pike's apartment at Cambridge University in England, where the bishop was studying. Most of these events were witnessed by—besides Pike himself—his secretary and a clergyman, the Rev. David Barr. One morning all the clocks stopped at exactly 8:19— the probable time, translated into Cambridge time, that the younger Pike had killed himself. Then saftey pins began turning up throughout the apartment, bent open to the angle made by the hands of a clock at 8:19. Books having some connection with the dead son appeared in locations other than their accustomed places. Hymnals and prayer books were found open on verses having eternal life as their theme. Once, while Pike, Barr, and the secretary were working in the apartment, there was a commotion in a closet. Pike quickly opened the door; no one was there, but the closet was a shambles of scrambled clothing. "If only," a visitor remarked on one occasion, "something of this sort would happen in the direct presence of witnesses." Immediately, in full view of the three witnesses present, the younger Pike's shaving mirror left the top of the bureau he had used while visiting his father, and floated gently to the floor.

When word of these happenings reached Mervyn Stockwood, Bishop of Southwark and a student of psychic phenomena, Stockwood surmised that Pike's son was desperately trying to establish communication with his father. Stockwood put Pike in touch with a medium, Mrs. Edna Twigg. Mrs. Twigg did not know who her new sitter was, but gave Pike messages he accepted as being from his dead son. The Rev. John Pierce-Higgins, who accompanied Pike as a witness, said James, Jr., through the medium, expressed regret for his suicidal act. He didn't mean to hurt anybody and wished he hadn't done it. He'd been under stress at examination time, "said something about drugs" (Pierce-Higgins) and guessed his mind had just cracked— couldn't face up to things all on his own. He'd had a premonition that "something terrible was going to happen" when he'd left his father at the airport. He expressed his affection for his father, and also his resentment over "the way they've been kicking you around"—referring to the disapproval by orthodox churchmen of some of Pike's theological ideas.

More than a year after all this, in September, 1967, events conspired to bring Bishop Pike and myself together. Allen Spraggett, religious editor of the Toronto *Star*, had written a book on psychic phenomena. Pike and I had been invited to speak on television as part of the publication-day publicity. At the Canadian Broadcasting Corporation's Toronto station, Pike fell in step beside me and said he'd like, if it could be arranged, to have a sitting sometime. We had previously agreed that a seance would be a good thing, but had not arranged a definite release date for the transcript. "What's the matter with right now?" I said. We went into the studio and made the tape that was later shown, in part, on the major United States and Canadian television networks.

An abundance of fresh material came through Fletcher, not only from Pike's son, but from other discarnates who had known the bishop. The younger Pike identified the drug he had previously mentioned as LSD—it had been another LSD tragedy. He had "got mixed up with the thing" in California, at college and had fallen in with some of the same crowd on his return to New York. The suicide had been the result of a "bad trip."

After the Pike seance, telephone calls were made immediately, to persons as far apart as Los Angeles and London, to check the discarnates' statements. One of the more interesting bits of the "trivial" variety had to do with two long-deceased pet cats. It suggests something that has long been speculated about in parapsychological lore—that animals as well as humans may survive death.

"There's an old gentleman here," Fletcher said to Pike during the seance, "who's with your son on the other side. He wants you to check out something that will prove his identity. He has two cats with him that once were pets of his son, who bears the same name he does—Donald MacKinnon. The present MacKinnon now lectures at Cambridge. James, Jr. used to drop in at his lectures." On the long-distance phone to Cambridge MacKinnon, who, it turned out, makes a hobby of cats, at once remembered the specific two Fletcher referred to. "That's extraordinary," he exclaimed, "I did have two pet cats—a black one and a grey one—when I was a boy. One disappeared some time before my father's death, the other acted strangely on the day of his funeral."

Fletcher spoke of "an elderly man of Slavic and Jewish background" who helped James, Jr., make his adjustment to the "other side." "Correct," said Bishop Pike, "Jim's maternal grandfather was a Russian Jew." Fletcher had said: "A man somewhat older than yourself, a university chaplain—Louis Pitt—says you'll remember him. They tried twice to make a bishop of him but failed." "It checks," said Pike. "Louis Pitt was my predecessor as chaplain at Columbia. He had poor luck in the matter of elevation to bishop—always a bridesmaid, never a bride." Another predecessor of Pike's—Karl Block, former Bishop of California—came on, through Fletcher, to identify himself and describe certain real estate transactions he had handled for his church that presumably only he could know about in any detail. Finally James, Jr., told about "a delightful elderly lady named Carol—Carol Rede—with whom you were associated at the cathedral (of St. John the Divine in New York). She asks that you look up her brother, a retired major living in Carmel, when you go back to California." "That was a shocker," Pike said. "I remember Carol Rede well, but didn't know she had died!"

After the seance there were the questions usually asked on such occasions—as to whether I might have picked up all this information by researching published materials, or by reading the minds of living persons. "I don't think so," Pike answered. "Some of the material was of such an intimately personal nature it had to be erased from the film. It certainly could not have been published and still is not published. Yet it checked out"—though understood in its full significance only by the Bishop himself. "Some details that proved correct were definitely beyond anything I could have known in my conscious mind—and I suspect, in some cases, in my unconscious."

An End to the Fear of Death

7

I have seen many people transformed by release from fear of death, through the final settling of their doubts about survival, that I marvel such relief is not more generally enjoyed. Men and women crushed by grief or crippled by the meaninglessness of a purely materialist existence have resumed enthusiastic living. Clergymen near despair at accepting pay for expounding doctrines they no longer believed have come alive again as centers of confidence and strength, preaching the message of continuing life with absolute conviction.

A general emancipation from the searing grip of this most fearsome of all dreads would free tremendous human energies for the creative tasks of life. And there is no *rational* reason for delaying any longer a general enjoyment of this immeasurable benefit. A hundred years of careful research has established the essential fact of survival to the satisfaction of all who approach the evidence with a free mind. Three thousand years of demonstration by prophets, saints, and heroes has suggested the capacity for expanded living that results when a human being sets aside his fear of death. There is no longer, I repeat, any rational reason to consider biological death a final end, or to fear it. Certain irrational factors, however, continually get in the way.

Not the least of these is the inhibiting influence of the spectacle of those in the throes of a profound grief. There is something about grief—perhaps its revelation of our universal interdependency—that repels that part of our minds which is ordinary, workaday, and self-centered. Since so many of those seeking the truth about survival have experienced or are experiencing bereavement, there is a tendency of the public, not wanting to be reminded of its physical mortality, to turn its eyes away.

I am not certain that people who seek endless seances in order to regain the habitual company of departed loved ones are doing the right thing. Here, it seems to me, the ordinary earth rules apply. Extreme dependency of any kind is generally recognized as a restricting influence on character development. There is a time, even in physical life, for the individual to break loose from old supports and make it on his own. Yet some people find it unusually hard to face up to the facts of life—and of death. Death is an irrevocable transition to a new environment, a leaving behind, despite the possibility of occasional brief returns, of familiar places, people, things, and activities. This parting is in some cases traumatic to those left behind; the wound seems never to heal; the death-fact cannot be accepted as one of the shocks of existence.

Many authorities have commented on this resistance to difficult truths. "We do not want to know our limitations, or the suffering and disappointment in store for us," writes George Lawton.

We want the solution to come from without, painlessly; we spurn any suggestion which requires our own slow, laborious efforts made in normal, daylight ways. However, the most efficient reaction to defeat contains much candor and little fear; failure simply makes the individual stop and take stock of himself. Evaluation and constructive thinking often result in a favorable modification of the individual's qualities. Though success still may not crown his efforts there is marked improvement in his ability to handle defeat. Others, instead of taking this difficult route, seek for a magic carpet to carry them instantly to their heart's desire. Eventually they realize that what seemed to be a shortcut through the psychic jungle turns out to be a blind alley.[1]

The death of someone with whom we have been long and closely associated leaves a vacuum in our lives that sometimes seems almost intolerable. The stream of psychic energy once directed into that person temporarily has no object. New objects—other persons or interests—need to be found. The person who has died leaves an image in the minds of those who knew him. For a time, the accustomed psychic energy is shunted into this image. But as new energy outlets are found, the image fades—life goes on. "Time heals," we say—the shock of bereavement is sustained, the depth of grief is survived. Finally there is left not an image but the memory of an image, or, as Lawton says, "a poignant, reflective sadness."

I have always considered the helping of bereaved persons to normal recovery from grief as one of my functions as a medium and an important part of my ministry. My higher purpose, however, is to teach and demonstrate survival, not as fuel for neurosis but as objective fact. People have a right to know the kind of universe they live in. The thing that heals is simply the truth.

One of the factors too seldom acknowledged is the hidden satisfaction, after grief has passed, with the situation just as it is. Even if we were certain that Granma Jones and Uncle Harry live on, would we really want to join them, or have them join us? Does the thought that we may eventually have to make peace with Grampa Miller—or with Mom and Dad—bring us pleasure or unease? Along with concern for the "dead" there is also a profound disinterest in them, extending on occasion to active revulsion. Death, to some, means a corpse and no more.

At the other extreme are the people who make a permanent institution of their grief. I have known parents who keep a room in their house for a long-departed child just as he left it, have a chair for him at table, keep his clothes in his closet and bureau. I am not convinced that this kind of thing is putting the fact of survival to its best use; it smacks too much of neurotic clinging. In physical life, when a child grows up and is on his own we encourage him, restricting our ties to not-too-frequent polite visits, with words of comfort when needed. We should not do less for him, or more, when the scene of his activities is transferred to the world of discarnates.

At this point I must remind my readers that besides being a medium I am also a Christian minister. To become more interested in discarnates than in God is, from the viewpoint of Christian theology, just as idolatrous as any other kind of inordinate attachment. For those who are religious skeptics, the same truth may be stated in nonecclesiastical terms: too great concentration on particulars puts one out of touch with the restorative power of the great universals.

Two things are absolutely essential to the overcoming of the fear of death. The first is to achieve conviction of survival of human personality after biological death by honest confrontation with the evidence. The second is to sustain this conviction against the eroding forces brought to bear on it by a materialist society. These two things accomplished, the truth of survival becomes part of one's core belief—like gravitation, one of the assured certainties of the universe. The two aspects of belief, emotional and intellectual, go together. Without the emotional support of immediately experienced phenomena, intellectual doctrine is likely to be sterile.

In such matters it is very hard to go it alone. We need the support of others who also have become aware of the death-transcending reality. Throughout human history this comradeship has been almost an essential to enduring freedom from man's central fear. It has been my good fortune to participate in just such a supportive movement in our own country and our own time. Called Spiritual Frontiers Fellowship, it now has a membership that is nationwide and growing.

The real impetus for SFF came from the author and leader in international Christianity, Dr. Sherwood Eddy. After producing thirty-nine books, Eddy wrote one in 1950 that was distinctly and dramatically different. For fourteen years, convinced that the promise of immortality was at the very core of Christianity, yet uncertain about the evidence, he had made his main concern the personal investigation of psychic phenomena that seemed to point to the possibility of an afterlife. At last unshakeably convinced, he offered his remarkable volume, *You Will Survive After Death*, as his contribution to the spread of the good news.

Dr. Eddy's name commanded world-wide respect, and his book had a tremendous impact on Christian laymen and clergymen throughout America. Many of them had heard of Spiritualism and perhaps read something about psychic phenomena, but this book carried conviction.

The slim volume by Sherwood Eddy brought together others throughout America who had been traveling a parallel path. One was Alson Smith, Methodist minister and

author of *Religion and the New Psychology,* who long had
felt that psychical truth held the key to renewing the lost
vitality of the churches. Paul L. Higgins, pastor of Hyde
Park Methodist Church in Chicago, had often discussed
pyschic matters with me on my trips to that city. W. H.
Leach, editor of the influential *Church Management,*
added his voice to the growing sentiment. S. E. Hening,
a Virginia businessman, brought back from one of his trips
recent word that a Churches' Fellowship for Psychical
Study had just been formed in England. Marcus Bach,
professor of religion at the State University of Iowa, together with former college president Albin Bro and his
author-wife Margueritte, added further enthusiastic voices.
Needless to say, I gave the movement my own unstinted
support. Having repeatedly crossed the country, talking
with ministers (among thousands of other people) and
giving seances in (among other places) churches and sem-
inaries, I had long sensed a need for some kind of national
organizing and directing influence.

In March, 1956, an organization meeting arbitrarily
limited to a hundred people was held in Chicago. People
from places as widely separated as Massachusetts and California, Oregon and Texas, ministers and laymen from Baptist, Congregational, Disciples, Episcopal, Reformed,
Quaker, Lutheran, Methodist, and Presbyterian churches
created the new fellowship. The assemblage adopted a
name—suggested by Mrs. Bro—and elected Rev. Paul Higgins first President. The Rev. Edmond G. Dyett, a Ph.D.
in psychology, provided headquarters space in his roomy
Evanston home and became full-time executive director.
A first year's program was approved and set in motion.
Since then the Fellowship has grown until religion-oriented
psychic groups now function in every section of the country. The Rev. George Wright became SFF's second President. The third and current President is William Rauscher,

an Episcopal rector of Woodbridge, N.J. Through its wide-spread group meetings and its magazine *Gateway*, SFF is introducing new thousands to the known unknown, cementing the certainty that brings an end to the fear of death.

My conviction, as I have said, is that intellectualization alone can never be more than a preliminary to releasing the emotion—comprehending love—that displaces that other emotion which has for so long been a plague to mankind: fear. Emotions of these dimensions, as I hope presently to show, involve not the mind alone but the whole being.

Those Tremendous Trivia

8

Mediumistic messages purporting to be from the dead have often been criticized on grounds that their content is trivial. If it is really the departed who are communicating, it is asked, why do they waste golden moments in idle chitchat or family gossip? Should not such rare opportunities be utilized for loftier themes? If there really is another world awaiting us after death, we have an almost excruciating longing to know what it is like. Why are we so seldom told? Why are we so often loaded with information of negligible importance while the great questions go begging?

It is a point deserving the most earnest consideration, and one which has received the careful attention of the best minds of psychical research. Several explanations have been offered. One of them, cleverly demonstrated early in this century by Columbia University's famous philosophy professor, James H. Hyslop, has been described by Louis Anspacher, one of his students who later became prominent as an author and playwright.

Hyslop had a telegraph line set up connecting two widely separated buildings on the Columbia campus, and posted skilled telegraphers at each end. While he took up a post at one end, a number of his students gathered at the other. One of the students was Anspacher. The purpose of the experiment was to determine what kind of communication would provide Hyslop with the kind of evidence that would enable him to say definitely which of his students was sending the message.

> When it was my turn [wrote Anspacher] I mentioned the remarkable fact that Royce, a Hegelian, James, a pragmatist, and Münsterberg, a materialist, were all on the same faculty of philosophy at Harvard at the same time. Then I discussed Bergson and the position of the institutionalists in modern philosophy. All to no purpose; Hyslop could not guess who was at the other end of the wire. But when I telegraphed the following: "Coming up in the Amsterdam Avenue car, you and I discussed Bergson's *Creative Evolution*. The conductor was amused at our barbarous French. We both tried to pay the fare. Your dime dropped into the mat." At this trivial communication, Hyslop promptly telegraphed back, "Anspacher."[1]

No other human being ever born had shared exactly these experiences, in exactly this order, with Hyslop; thus he was able to say without any doubt or reservation where the message had originated. A great many of the messages that come through Fletcher and myself are of just this agent-identifying kind.

The writer-editor-professor Jerome Ellison has told me of another sequence of this kind. It began with the first of a series of sittings he had with me while researching psychic phenomena. The dialog between himself and Fletcher, Ellison says, went something like this:

"There is someone here who is very much interested in you. Name of Burch."

"Yes?"

"Seems that he knew you when you were a boy."

"I once had a Sunday-school teacher named Mr. Burch. A fine man."

"There is something about a rabbit. Some connection with a white rabbit."

"I had a white rabbit once when I was a boy, but it had nothing to do with Mr. Burch."

"Well, I see this white rabbit, as related somehow to you and Mr. Burch. A bunny. Bunny. Was Mr. Burch's nickname 'Bunny'?"

"Certainly not. He was much too dignified to have a nickname."

"Well," said Fletcher, sounding a little frustrated, "see if you can check it out."

He then went on with messages for other sitters. More than a year later, on a visit to his boyhood home, Ellison related the incident to his aging mother.

"You mean you don't *remember?!*" she exclaimed. "The white rabbit was an Easter present given you one year by your Sunday-school teacher, Mr. Burch."

"There are only two possible explanations," Ellison told me. "Either it was Mr. Burch identifying himself, or you making up a tale out of material you snitched tele-pathically from my memory—or, in this case, forgettery. Of the two, the Mr. Burch hypothesis seems by far the most likely. Of all the material stored on my memory-tape, why would you pick this particular item—unless you were nudged to it by some psychic entity who wanted you to pick just that and nothing else? Children, I have noticed, are more likely to remember an exciting gift than to remember its donor. "Who gave me the Bat Man outfit?" is a common question even a few days after Christmas, at thank-you note-writing time. Doubtless it was so in my own case. Without my mother's recollection I would have missed entirely the importance of this very evidential message. I have had only one rabbit in my entire life. It was given to me by Mr. Burch. No living person knew it but my mother, who had never mentioned it from the time of the gift until told of the message. It establishes to my complete satisfaction the all-important fact that the long-"dead" Mr. Burch, wherever he may be, is in a position, when circumstances are right, to communicate with living people.

One of my own earliest psychic experiences, dating from a time even before my teaming up with Fletcher, revolved around this sort of identification message. When I was in college, several of my fraternity brothers took an interest in psychic matters, seeking out psychics and fortune-tellers whenever they had the opportunity, and comparing results. One of them, named Joe, contracted a fatal case of pneumonia. When the doctors had given up hope for him, he called me to his side and, between his last struggles to breathe, said, "If I can get back I'll give you proof."

Months later I attended a Spiritualist camp meeting while on vacation in Michigan. The clairvoyant said she had a message for me and described Joe, though she could not get his name. The message was not entirely clear but it was something about dynamite. I could in no way connect Joe with dynamite, and so forgot the whole business. A year or so later another psychic in another state went through exactly the same routine—and a year after that a third medium brought Joe to me again. The medium insisted Joe was saying a word that sounded like dynamite, but was not precisely that word. My friend was now asking, the medium said, that I go through the word with him syllable by syllable each of us taking alternative syllables. Immediately I understood. The secret password of our fraternity was *Dynamus*, exchanged alternate syllable-by-syllable among the brothers, along with the secret grip. The password changed each year; the year Joe died it was *Dynamus*.

The persistence of the communication, combined with the fact that nobody knew the password but the members of that small group at that small college that single year, convinced me beyond any question that it was actually Joe making good his promise to give me evidence of survival if it turned out really to be so.

This, then, is the distinguishing character of many highly evidential messages—a dime dropped on the floor mat in a trolley car, a small gift given and received during a forgotten stretch of childhood, a bit of ritualistic hocus-pocus from a long-dispersed fraternal group. Trivial? In a way, yes. But always trivial in the particular way of establishing past any possibility of mistake that the message originates with one particular psychic entity associated with a person assumed to be dead, and with no other.

In my opinion, this circumstance alone does not wholly account for the casual small-talk tone of so many medium-transmitted communications. I would once again remind my readers of two circumstances newcomers to psychic matters tend to forget—discarnates are people, and seances are semipublic occasions attended by persons of varied backgrounds who are for the most part strangers to one another.

Even among flesh-and-blood people in everyday earth life, small talk has its uses as a social lubricant. The insurance salesman does not hawk insurance in the middle of a funeral service. The Lochinvar does not make love at a public lecture. The preacher does not deliver a sermon at a ball game. We do not usually talk politics during a wedding ceremony. The universally accepted convention for communications on all these occasions—and a million others, including seances—is small talk.

Besides, most people have areas of rigid opinion of such explosive character that if touched upon even casually they blow up—blasting as they blow whatever social occasion (such as a seance) may be in progress. With Uncle Mark it's politics, with Aunt Hattie religion, with Cousin Tom, the possibility of an afterlife, with niece Susie the relative appeal of current TV performers.

In acknowledgment of this hazard, most earthside social gatherings are dominated by unimportant remarks about the weather, the state of one's physical health, and the standings of various athletic teams. It is the mark of a most discriminating social sense, it seems to me, that discarnates so often tread nimbly among subjects which accomplish their main purpose without marring the cordiality of the occasion.

And just what is this main purpose? It has been so well said by Anspacher I cannot do better than quote him again. "In these communications we should not expect important descriptions of the future life. In reality, such descriptions are not important. We must bear in mind that our whole vocabulary is earthbound and three-dimensional. When we consider the difficulties of communication it is marvelous that we get anything at all, no matter how trivial. Every word we use is jammed full of our earthly experience. Discarnate spirits, if there are such, may as yet have no vocabulary to describe a world they have never before experienced." Would you, in this world, ask a doctoral dissertation from a newborn infant? "So possibly all they can do is say: 'Hello, I am here.' "[2]

Actually, there is a certain deep wisdom shown by discarnates in not trying for profundities when conditions are not right. Right conditions do sometimes occur, however, and, as I will show in the next chapter, it is a matter of record that what Anspacher calls "important descriptions of the future life" have been received. Meanwhile, discarnates' favorite method of signaling to mankind, with indefatigable persistence, the unassailable reality of life after death continues to be the citing of minor items of remembered experience that uniquely identify the communicator—that say, "Hello, I am here!"

Such messages come through Fletcher and me in truly astonishing quantity and variety. Another evidential quality, closely related to unique trivia but not quite the same, is something that might be called the "sense of personality." This was mentioned to me by Jerome Ellison after a later sitting with me, during which Ellison received greetings from a former editorial associate, George Grant.

Shortly after Ellison had left the magazine that employed them both (*Reader's Digest*) Grant died of a bacterial infection.

What impressed me with the authenticity of the message was not its factual content. It is just possible— though not at all likely—that the barebones facts might have been gathered by prolonged investigation and research. What absolutely could not have been faked by anybody who had not known George well and at the same time been a gifted mimic—and I knew with practically 100 per cent certainty that neither Ford nor Fletcher had known him at all, much less seen him in action long enough to do a perfect imitation—was the precise quality of friendly, sometimes almost affectionate earnestness-combined-with-matter-of-factness with which he had been in the habit of talking to me. Even if this could have been imitated, nobody could have caught the exact tone of backhall office chitchat that went on when we worked together, except through a long exposure the Fletcher-Ford team could never have had. It was unquestionably my old co-worker George.

A similar quality—a particular flavor of personality combined with a style of family-talk prevailing only within his family—was present, Ellison says, when he communicated with his son, Jerome III (killed accidentally in 1952) during a sitting held in 1956.

Discarnates communicating through my mediumship have shown—according to the scripts, tapes, typed transcripts, notes, and letters given me after sittings during which I am in trance and unconscious—a great variety of ways to indicate their identity. Mrs. Robert M. Conner of Cambridge, Ohio, has reported a sitting, held in Cleveland in 1967 and attended by a number of witnesses including her husband, Dr. and Mrs. Naldo Moss, and Mr. Robert Hoyle, during which Fletcher brought messages laden with an unusually high content of verifiable factual information.

"I am a genealogist," writes Mrs. Conner. "At the time of the sitting I was compiling a book, *Pioneer Families of Guernsey County, Ohio*. Several locations where pioneer families had lived back in the early 1700's could not be found." During the sitting, Fletcher introduced discarnates who "told where they had lived and named the county. With this clue we were able to locate the early county records and trace the relationships."

On one occasion a discarnate, through Fletcher, dragged a family skeleton out of its closet. This was recorded by Frances M. Bolling during a sitting held in the spring of 1955, attended by herself and six others.

Fletcher asked, "Is there an A.B.B. here?" A.B.B. was not present but I knew her and said so. Her brother L. wanted to get a message to her, so I took it all down, and the next day took it to her . . . I approached the matter delicately: "Do you have a brother L.?" She smiled with pride and told me about her talented brother who had died. Did he have something to do with the furniture you now have in your home? He did, and she told me about it.

Then I asked, "Did your brother drink?" No, he was a wonderful person, etc.

"Then he didn't die of too much drink?" A.B.B. looked horrified.

"Did your brother ever leave his wife and go off with another woman?"

"Goodness, no."

By this time I was confused and embarrassed before my honorable and highly respected friend. I told her the whole story of Arthur Ford's having been here, of the sitting, of all her brother was supposed to have said, including his remark, "Though I went to Mexico with Helen I never really loved her. I always loved my wife and I so want her to know it."

At this point A.B.B broke in with great emphasis: "I always *knew* he never loved Helen." The family skeleton having been discovered, she now corroborated every detail, except that the cause of death had not been given as alcoholism but as "something else."

When "L.'s" widow heard of the sitting, she came to Frances Bolling for a firsthand account.

Discarnates who had a sense of humor in the flesh-and-blood life do not lose it, and particularly like to recall running family jokes. Here is part of a tape made during a sitting in my Philadelphia apartment in March, 1965, when eleven persons from Elizabethtown, Pa., came for a seance previously arranged.

FLETCHER: I have to put it into words. I don't get words, we don't have words over here, just ideas. He shows me something that looks like a bottle of beer. Whether it's wine, beer or something . . . Is there someone alcoholic? Who is Ella?

FISHER: Ella is his wife.

FLETCHER: Is she an alcoholic?

FISHER: No.

FLETCHER: Well, he smiles (laughter by all) and he says—but I don't know what he's talking about, but anyhow he says she's on the earth plane.

CUSTER: Right.

FLETCHER: "If you see her tell her I came through and it's a joke between us." And I don't know what it is. He must have called her a boozer or something.

FISHER: Her maiden name was Boose or something like that.

FLETCHER: Oh, Boose—Booser. He smiles.

Mrs. Dorothy M. Forney of Elizabethtown appends the following explanatory note to this passage: "Ella is A. C. Baugher's widow, who is still living. We learned some time after the reading that there was a private joke between these two about her maiden name, which was Boaz. He often called her 'Boozer' as a joke, and took special delight in teasing Mrs. Baugher about being his 'boozer.' A joke it was indeed, since both were members of the Church of the Brethren."

Dr. M. Edmund Speare, a Ph.D. from Johns Hopkins, taught for many years at Harvard, became an editor with the Oxford University Press, and is a prolific author. His wife, Florence Lewis Speare, who died in 1965, had been a well-known playwright. Dr. Speare has written this comment on evidential detail:

I have had *six* sittings with the Rev. Arthur Ford, the first on March 12, 1966; the most recent on March 13, 1968. The veridical points and messages that, through Fletcher, Ford's control, have been poured upon me at these sittings—mainly from my wife, my parents, former university teachers like William James, academic colleagues who have passed on, my wife's discarnate relatives and my own—*have transformed my life!* Every word at these sittings was tape-recorded; hence, though for some messages it has taken me months to verify statements made to me, the great majority of them proved correct. Space permits my giving here only a very few of these "points" that were solely informative. Statements filled with affection, compassion, tenderness, which pervade these sittings I have omitted, for they are so personal that they have no place here. To pack as much as possible into this "report," I have had to condense the original statements given via Fletcher. Statements hereafter are always Fletcher's, as he hears the discarnates or reads their minds. Comments of mine are in parentheses or brackets.

1. "Florence says, 'There is a person here who knows about you: his name is David Little; he was Curator of the Harvard Theater Collection; he declares that all my plays, manuscripts, novels, letters from G. B. Shaw, Masefield, Lady Gregory, Yeats, and other worthies are to go to that Collection; he was Master of Adams House at Harvard. Did you know him?'" (Speare: No, I never heard of him. There was no Adams House in my Harvard days.) [*My comment*: Only three persons alive, at the time of this sitting, knew that the Harvard Curator of the Drama Collection had asked me for Florence's books and papers; that each unit was to be designated the *Florence Lewis Speare Memorial Collection*; that they were to be despatched nine days after this sitting

to Harvard; that the only three living persons who knew of this were John Mason Brown, the dramatic critic and lifelong friend of Florence's, who instigated this business by stimulating the Harvard Curator to write to me; the Curator; and I. After the registered packet had been received at Harvard and a wonderful letter of appreciation had been received by me from that Curator, I phoned her long distance and asked: "Who was David Little? Was he ever a Curator of the Harvard Drama Collection? What was his position at Harvard during his life there?" Her answers: "No, he was never the Curator, but he did much curatorial work during his life at Harvard; he died before I came here; he was much loved by all who knew him; he left a MS, on David Garrick, which the Harvard Press has published; he was Master of Adams House here—a House built long after you studied and taught at Harvard."]

2. "Your wife, Florence, had another name when she was younger—they used to call her Flora; but she seemed when young to have still another name—*Jean*. Did you know that?" (Speare: No, I didn't know that. I'll have to look it up.) [I did later: I found girlhood evidences that she had been called, at times, *Jean*.]

3. "Your wife shows me a picture of a corner of your living room; at left-center is a table; there is a lamp with a reddish shade; there is your chair to the right of that; behind you in the corner are shelves of books; the scene changes, and as you sit in that chair and read, whenever you look up, you look straight into her photograph." [*My comment*: This is an exact picture of our living room, my chair, the corner filled with bookcases, her secretaire near which she had her typewriter and worked; and as I turn to the left I look up into an enlargement of her beautifully noble face, a framed portrait 21 " by 19", over which hangs a fluorescent portrait-gallery

lamp, switched on throughout my waking hours. Mr.
Ford never visited this apartment, and never had this
corner or living room described to him. Since her "passing" I had moved into this smaller apartment, hence
this differs from the one she knew in life. It is evident
that she has visited this one often.]

4. "Your wife says she is gloriously happy. 'And you
are always writing, of course; never see you when you're
not writing. You are writing even now, and it's good.' "
[My comment: Again evidence of her presence in my
present apartment, and knowing what I am doing and
have been these many months. I am at work on a book
that is to be, God willing, a worthy biography of her
life and mine. Mr. Ford had never been told of this
except now, as I pass on to him this report.]

5. "There's someone here named Will Cuppy. He
wants to thank you for making him articulate, under-
standable, and he is grateful to you. Florence says she
didn't approve of him; she didn't dislike him, but she
didn't think he was worth bothering about." [My comment: Cuppy, former book editor of the then famous
New York Herald-Tribune, did two books with me:
World's Great Mystery Stories and World's Great De-
tective Stories. A brilliant and witty man, he was also a
dipsomaniac, and had to be urged on to do his literary
chores, daily. I had great influence on him. But, I had
completely forgotten these forty years, and now Florence for the first time reminds me that she once said to
me that she didn't think he was "worth bothering
about." Will Cuppy must have "died" some thirty years
ago.]

6. "She says you two went back to a ter-ter-centenary;
she shows the number 1936—'It's a college where we
met. While we were there we had a talk with some one
who wants to greet you. He's rather small; a funny-

looking man; used to wear highbutton shoes; has on a baggy, rumpled suit, shiny, of blue serge; he says to tell you that he is Uncle Fritz. Maybe *you* didn't call him that; you must have been more respectful than some of his other students. He says he is Frederick Robinson, and he holds up something called *Canterbury Tales*. He says to you: "I knew your wife long before I knew you." He used to climb mountains when he was younger. He says to you, "I am sure that with your renewed interest in life, and the real meaning of existence, you will probably live to be as old as I was." ' " [*My comment*: We went back in 1936 to Harvard's Tercentenary celebration. It was founded in 1636. I took three courses with Professor Robinson at Harvard: Middle English, Chaucer, and Anglo-Saxon. I remembered vaguely that my beloved wife once told me that she knew Robinson long before she had met me. To check on his comments to me I finally made contact with his only living nephew, living in Cambridge, Mass. He wrote me that (1) by his intimates and relatives his uncle was always called *Uncle Fritz*; (2) that he had been for years a member of the Appalachian Club and probably climbed mountains in his youth; (3) that he died at the age of ninety-five; (4) that in his later years he used the pockets of his suit as a kind of filing system, and there kept his personal papers; (5) that he did wear in his latest years custommade button shoes.]

Some discarnates, having once been convinced that biological death was a final end, were surprised, after "death," to find themselves still in business, and are eager and happy to recant their previous views. Mrs. Mary Southworth of West Lafayette, Indiana, gives the following account of a sitting with Fletcher and me in Chicago, 1960:

Arthur Ford brought through various relatives of mine and then said, "Here is Lark."

I said, "Lark? I don't know a Lark."

"It's Lark-Horowitz" (Karl Lark-Horowitz, head of Physics Department at Purdue University).

"Why, Fletcher, Lark-Horowitz is living."

"Well, he's over on this side, and he has a message for you to take to Big Robbie" (C. H. Robertson, very tall, retired Y.M.C.A. missionary in China, inventor, one-time teacher of physics at Purdue). "When he was living, Big Robbie would tell him about God and afterlife—that you did live on—but Lark said he didn't believe it, he thought you just died. But Big Robbie said no, you don't just die, you live on, and it's merely going through a door. And I didn't believe it. But will you please tell Robbie it's so. I am living, and teaching, and am so happy! I want to apologize to Big Robbie. He was so right, and tell him it is so much more wonderful than even he told me."

I was sure Professor Lark-Horowitz was living. I called up Professor Burr on the Purdue campus and asked, "Is Lark-Horowitz teaching at the university?"

"No," he said, "he died a couple of months ago." Big Robbie himself was very ill and died several weeks after this. I was able to repeat to him many times this message from Lark-Horowitz, which he liked to hear.

Sometimes, as the following three transcripts from my sittings suggest,[3] identification is established through personal intimacies or details of circumstances of death known only to the discarnate sender and incarnate receiver of the message.

First:

I get the name . . . Schleming.
Here.

Lucy comes to me. It seems she was a friend of yours, a sweetheart—I see you close together. She died in an accident on the 13th of . . . February.

13th of January.

13th of January. It was an automobile accident. You were with her.

Yes.

She tells me to tell you she heard you, even though she could not answer. You picked her up and held her in your arms and said, "It's Bill, Lucy, answer me, just one word!" Isn't that so?

Yes, every word.

She tells me to say she's waiting for you, that though you could not marry she is your wife and will join you when you come over. She was buried on a little hill in Hackensack.

A little hill, yes, but in Nyack.

I knew it was New Jersey. You put flowers on her grave on March 22nd and came here to communicate with her.

Yes.

You almost ran off the road coming here.

Yes. . . .

You mentioned her name at the time, whispering, "Lucy, dear."

Second:

This is from Anna to Herbert. Who is Anna?

My daughter.

In spirit.

Yes.

Anna tells me to tell Herbert it was Irene's sister who did it. She played the piano that afternoon. Would you understand that?

I have never seen you before, nor have you seen me. I have been looking for this for a long time, but this is the most marvelous proof I could ever have received. I have asked another famous medium but he said he could not answer it. We have wanted to know who played that afternoon and now we know. This is the most wonderful evidence I could ever have gotten. Thank you! Thank you!

Third:

I want to come to . . . you . . . Baxter. That is your name, is it not?

Yes. I get the names of two men, Hollaway and Leventritt, and a woman, Sterling. There was a group of twelve people in two roller coasters at an amusement resort. You were in the one behind.

Yes.

The first one went over and three persons in it were killed; the others were injured. One died since, but not as a result of the accident. Your own car was derailed.

Yes.

There are two types of cases that bring the psychic exceptional satisfaction—those which clearly result in helping desperate people, and those which result in acceptance of the facts of life-after-death by hardshelled skeptics. The helping of people in crisis hardly belongs in a chapter on trivia. But, since so many skeptics are enlightened by the kind of tremendous trivia that allow only one explanation, the second category is appropriate here. I have already mentioned the Lark-Horowitz case as an instance of scientific skepticism. Dr. Edward Bauman, pastor of the Foundry Methodist Church in Washington, provides an instance of what might be called religious skepticism.

"Four years ago," Dr. Bauman recently told reporters, "I went with a physician friend to see Arthur Ford. I went in a very skeptical frame of mind and was ready to poke holes in the whole business. Before the evening was over I was a devotee." I now number Dr. Bauman among my good friends. He is a member of the national executive council of Spiritual Frontiers Fellowship.

The case of Ruth Montgomery illustrates a skepticism that might be called the hardboiled journalistic type. Here's the story in her own words.

Shortly after I had written a newspaper series debunking mediums, Arthur Ford's arrival in Washington stirred my curiosity and I made an appointment to see him. I told him of my debunking series, and he would have been wise to show me to the door if he had anything to hide. Instead, he asked if I would like for him to see whether he could get anything for me through Fletcher. . . .

One of the gentlemen introduced by Fletcher persisted in talking about the troubles in Africa, particularly in the Congo. "He is very disturbed about something that is happening where he lived in Africa many years ago," the control relayed. "His name is Ed . . . no, no, it's Fred . . . Fred Bennett. He seems to have been an uncle. I think he was a preacher in Africa." I had never heard of him, and bluntly said so. Fletcher paused only momentarily before adding: "He says he didn't know you personally, but to ask your husband."

That evening when Bob came home from the office, I asked if he had ever heard of anyone named Fred Bennett.

"I had an aunt who married a Fred Bennett," he replied, "but he's been dead since I was a child. How did you hear of him?" Ignoring his question for the moment, I asked what Bennett had done for a living. I shall never forget his response: "He was a foreign missionary in the Congo. Why?" . . .

Fletcher said, "I have to get this name phonetically, because we don't use words over here. A man named Ida—no—Ina—no, but that's close, a three-letter word beginning with I. He's very fine, looks quite a bit like you. Must be your father."

I acknowledged that Dad's name was Ira, and Fletcher continued: "He sends you his love. Says he was quite ill before he came over, but then he came very suddenly. He didn't know it was that serious. He doesn't remember about dying, and says he hasn't found anyone over here who does. There is no dying. All of a sudden you're free, that's all. . . . He says . . . he enjoyed his funeral very much. It was beautiful and simple, but he wasn't dead. He had merely gotten rid of his sick body. He says give his love to your mother. Is there someone named Bertie? He keeps saying Bertie."

I replied that this was his nickname for my mother, Bertha. . . .

Fletcher then brought this message: "Your father says the most important story in the world for you to write is this: 'I live, and we are in a world of activity and growth. I couldn't be happy if idle.' " . . .

Fletcher next said that "a Clyde Wildman, who used to be connected with schools," wanted to tell me that "someone who once lived near you, in a street or town called Lafayette, has mysteriously disappeared, but he's over here now. He drowned. He was an official of some kind—seems to have been a judge." By then I was beginning to feel like an idiot child. I knew of no Wildman, nor of any disappearing judge since Crater, who was certainly not from Lafayette, Indiana, where I once lived briefly in my youth.

The next day I telephoned the Lafayette *Courier-Journal* to seek possible clues. No sooner had I lamely begun to explain the purpose of the call than editor George Lamb declared: "That would be Judge Lynn Parkinson, of course. He used to live in Lafayette, but was judge of the U.S. Court of Appeals in Chicago when he disappeared last fall." He said that despite an intensive FBI search through seven states, the only trace found of the judge was his hat and umbrella, lying on the shore of Lake Michigan near the Lakeshore Hotel. . . . The editor searched old city directories and found that Judge Parkinson, who had once been a university president, had indeed lived only a few blocks from my family in West Lafayette twenty-five years before. What neither the editor nor I could then know was that a few weeks later the judge's decomposed body would be found floating on Lake Michigan. . . .

During a later seance, Fletcher reminded me that at a sitting the previous year he had said that President Kennedy would be killed in a moving conveyance while away from the White House. I had forgotten it until I rechecked the tape recording. Now, only a month after the assassination, Fletcher flatly informed me that only one southern state would go uncommitted to the Democratic convention the following summer—Alabama —and that President Johnson would easily win election to a full term. . . .

A week before the election, on October 28, 1964, I received a telegram from Walter Voelker, an engineer-inventor who had attended a Ford seance in Philadelphia the evening before: "Harold Ickes via Ford predicts Goldwater electoral vote 43 minimum 52 maximum." The actual Goldwater electoral vote turned out to be 52. . . . The voice purporting to be JFK's placed the blame for the Bay of Pigs fiasco squarely on a still living person, and our involvement in Vietnam on another individual . . . but as there is no intent here to embarrass anyone this intriguing portion of the seance is being withheld.[4]

Fletcher's predictions have scored several other notable hits. In the same communication referred to above, giving the Goldwater electoral vote, there were strong hints of the Kennedy assassination and Johnson's declining to run in '68. These words are from the transcript: "Something about the election. But the tragic thing about it is—and this I want you to have on record but don't talk about it—we are quite convinced here that in the next eight years there will be three different men in the White House. Now that means that two of the people who will probably go into the White House will not be there at the end of eight years. And the one who goes in at this election will probably not be there at the end of his term. We don't like to tell you this, but it's here and we want it on record, you understand?"

The following is an excerpt of a tape made by Fletcher on April 16, 1967 (Martin Luther King was assassinated in April, 1968):

FLETCHER: There are several people here . . . Carlson says, I am going to make a prediction which I want you to note very carefully. He says someone with a name similar to Martin Luther, but speaking about a colored man. There is a plan which is almost completed and which will be carried out. I don't like the plan. But the Reverend Martin Luther King is marked for assassination. It will not be too long.

JOHN: Can he tell me who has marked him for assassination?

FLETCHER: No. I picked up the mental image of it. He'll be assassinated. That's all I can see.

JEAN: Can it be stopped?

FLETCHER: No.

JOHN: Can he see when, Fletcher?

FLETCHER: No, not in detail. I only see that it is part of the picture. On these precognitive things you only pick up a plan.

JOHN: But it is going to happen?

FLETCHER: Yes.

Again—and this is on record in the December 14, 1967 issue of the Philadelphia *Inquirer*—Fletcher relayed advance word of the Vietnam peace talks.

I'd like to end this chapter as I began it—with the good Professor Hyslop, who, as a faithful officer of the American Society for Psychical Research until his death in 1920, did so much to acquaint the concerned with the dimension of life-beyond-life. It also allows me to introduce Miss Gertrude Tubby, a former secretary of ASPR, an assistant to Hyslop, and a generous guide to my own explorations during my early days in this work.

Several years ago, two editors of a publishing house arranged for a sitting—a man we'll call Smith and a woman we'll call Jones. Fletcher brought Hyslop on, and the professor inquired about the progress in their publishing house of "his book"—an account of "some of my work with Miss Tubby since my death." When informed the editors hadn't seen the manuscript, Hyslop assured them they'd have it shortly.

Two weeks later Jones arrived for another sitting, having meanwhile received a six-hundred page tome she called "Hyslop." The discarnate was waiting to be first to appear during the seance.

"I haven't finished your manuscript," said Jones.

"I know, I know," Hyslop said, "it's hard to read anything with so many handwritten insertions. But in a couple of days you'll be meeting Tubby and you two can take it from there." Two days later, Jones found herself passing through Montclair, New Jersey—on an unexpected trip—and phoning Miss Tubby for an appointment to see her at her home in that town.

"That's Professor Hyslop," said Miss Tubby on being told of the incident. "He never gives up."

Trivial, all this? Perhaps so, but trivia of a certain carefully calculated grandeur. They tell us things—things of transcendant importance—with a precision and a certainty that could never be conveyed with ornate rhetoric or theoretical abstractions.

Things Not So Trivial

9

One time a Cincinnati newspaper columnist, hearing I was in town, wrote that he'd come to hear me if I'd "produce Moses or Jeremiah," but he had no time for the kind of back-fence gossip that usually came over. I retorted that Fletcher and I would be glad to bring in Moses or Jeremiah —*if* he would promise to rule whether or not the discarnates who came through actually *were* these dignitaries.

Around the questions raised in this little contretemps revolves the whole future of psychic—and, as we shall presently see—psychological research. Obviously, if communication with discarnates is to have meaning in any fundamental sense, the identity of communicators must be established beyond any reasonable doubt. This, we have discovered, is best accomplished through revelations of unique and personal detail.

Once the fact of survival is established, however, many of our profoundest questions still remain unanswered— among them the columnist's querulous query. Why, indeed, do we not more often hear from famous figures of history and legend? If survival is a fact, what do we survive *for?* What's it like to have survived biological death? What does one do, and why? Once one is set up in this new condition, what sort of future is there? How about such once-familiar life elements as food, shelter, sleep, work, entertainment, sex, business, social life? How about earth-level prestige, monetary and otherwise—do you really "take it with you" or not? Can the dog-lover's favorite collie go along some day? What have the great thinkers of the past got to say about mankind's current predicaments? Why don't communicating discarnates spend more time on these major questions and less on personal small talk?

These are proper questions. There are, one may discover with a little delving, satisfying answers to them all.

Some of these questions answer themselves as soon as one returns to the human factor. Discarnates, we must remember, are people. So are the incarnate sitters at earthside seances. Some people, trivial by nature, never ask deeply significant questions of discarnate visitors and so, of course, never get significant answers. They simply are not interested in big issues. A certain personality type, often manifested in newspaper reporters and casual intellectuals, has become all too familiar to me. Its typical representative will attend a seance, sit glumly and silently, or speak only when spoken to, and then, if a message has been received, go out with a glow of surprise. "What do you know, I talked with old Aunt Hattie the other evening!" Then, the initial excitement past, he will forget entirely what the fact that he could talk with Aunt Hattie actually *means*—in terms of the total structure of things— and sit down to write a cold and quarrelsome piece about the lack of profundity in spirit messages.

Discarnates are also people and can also be trivial. The mere fact of a person's abandoning his alpha body to live solely in his beta body does not at once endow him with gifts of comprehension he didn't have before. In the seance situation we must always bear in mind the astronomical differences in human personalities on both sides of the medium—incarnate and discarnate. These differences run the intellectual gamut from near-moron to genius. Morally, they range from saint to criminal, from altruistic self-giving to ruthless self-centeredness, from killer to healer, from friend to foe, from love to hate. Linguistically they include all the languages of earth. Culturally they include every conceivable human circumstance of life. Some of these differences are so great the communication gap cannot be bridged.

This, I repeat, is universally part of the human condition; one does not need to wait to become a discarnate to know it—although as the New Testament points out in the parable of Lazarus and Dives, it is well known to discarnates. Dives, the rich sybarite now discarnate, wanted Lazarus, the beggar of earth now in Abraham's bosom, to get word back to his brothers to amend their self-indulgent lives. If they would not heed Moses, was the reply, they would not heed one returned from the dead. Between Dives and Lazarus was "a great gulf fixt." "I didn't have to die," a friend of mine told me recently, "to find out about the great gulf. When I changed my politics from moderate right to moderate left my one-time friends fell away beyond the gulf. We still communicate, but only in remote nods and brief greetings during unavoidable confrontations—empty of content."

Mediums too, let us not forget, are people, possessing, in addition to their unusually developed gift of communication, all the vagaries of character known to people in general. They range from the rigorously honest to the appallingly deceitful. I have known mediums who would gladly produce Jesus, George Washington, Abraham Lincoln, Joshua, or Moses on request. The fact that all these beings spoke in the same Southern drawl and shared the same Bible-belt fundamentalist convictions and had an extremely narrow range of local interests bothered the medium not at all. It would certainly cause some doubts to arise, however, in the mind of even the most sympathetic psychical researcher. Take the language issue alone. Few people anywhere on earth—and almost no Americans —could understand the vernacular Greek, Latin, and Hebrew dialects used by the great figures of the New Testament.

Does this mean that the persons known to us through history and legend never communicate? I think not. The world-renowned theologian Paul Tillich was once present at a service of spiritual healing during which there was no attempt at mediumistic communication. At one point Dr. Tillich said, "I sense the presence of Francis of Assissi."[1] Now merely to "sense the presence" is not enough to convince the scientific researcher, no matter how distinguished the sensor. The evidence certainly is not conclusive.

But it is, I offer, suggestive. When a person endowed with the great gifts of Dr. Tillich—his unassailable probity, his meticulous scholarship, his clear and almost hardheaded approach to spiritual matters—senses a presence, the experience should not be too hastily brushed aside.

Shifting our view to the other side, would such an appearance be characteristic of Francis? A case could be made. When incarnate, he used a blend of Latin vulgate and Italian nobody present on this occasion would understand. The intelligent and realistic Francis would have better sense—and better manners—than to jabber in a lingo incomprehensible to the people he loved and wanted to serve. This need not mean that he was without means of expressing himself. Dr. Tillich's sense of a presence, while not conclusive, is worthy of note.

Another important factor in this discussion is the sometimes negative effect of the passage of time. Take the case of the French-speaking Napoleon, an historic figure who frequently turns up in questionable seances—sometimes speaking a type of hillbilly English he was never known to use in his incarnate state. Suppose, merely for the sake of discussion, that Napoleon, after thinking things over for a century or so and broadening his experience in areas he had never explored during his earth life, became a pacifist. Would he, if he had something important to communicate to incarnate mankind, use a name remembered as belonging to a ruthless militarist? If he did, would his communication be credited? Even if he carefully explained his change of heart, would he not almost certainly be regarded by the skeptical—even by the merely cautious—as an imposter?

Or take Oliver Lodge, whom I knew. At the zenith of his career, Lodge was one of the world's most respected physicists. Physics has made enormous forward strides since Lodge's time on earth. There is no reason to think he has not kept abreast of these new developments in his field, or even gone beyond them. If he wanted to communicate some of these new findings, would he use a name associated with theories now outmoded? If he did, would not the content of his message be discredited as originating from a thinker whose ideas were long outdated? Or discredited for the opposite reason—that "Lodge was never known to think in these terms"?

These are difficult questions. They are so difficult, in fact, that many scientists fight shy of them because of their very difficulty. This, I suggest, is unscientific. The proper scientific response to a difficult problem is not simply to refuse to look at it. It is rather to look at it with more than usual care, and to approach it with means appropriate to its solution.

A great deal of impressive material—including answers

to such questions as "what kind of life will we lead after we have 'passed on'?"—has already accumulated and awaits scientific evaluation. Some of the most intelligent of this, probably for reasons suggested above, has been brought by discarnates who prefer to remain pseudonymous and identify themselves by such names as "Imperator," "Rex," "Invisible," or simply "Communicator." Some of these, we have reason to think, have been quite distinguished earth personages. Given the proper circumstances of intelligent and large-minded sitters, a reasonably competent and reasonably honest medium, and an outstanding earth-mind—or group of minds—now well established in the discarnate world, and messages of the most profound content can result. Sometimes, as has happened in my own mediumship, the discarnate gives his full and proper legal name.

Before going on to this material it is necessary once more to remind ourselves, and in slightly different contexts, that people, whether incarnate or discarnate, are people and share all the well-known characteristics of people.

Bearing in mind this universal human quality of "peopleness," let us suppose you are now twenty-nine years old and married. Do you possess the same inventory of ideas, needs, interests, and ambitions you had when you were nine years old and unmarried? Of course not; you have developed, and your development has brought change—*perhaps even evolutionary change*. Or suppose you move to a new city. Will your estimate of it be the same when you have been there six years as it was when you'd been there six days? Most likely not. As you come to know the place, its possibilities, resources, and people, your attitude toward it evolves.

One more "suppose." Suppose we put the following people on a plane to Chicago—a housewife, a stenographer, a doctor, a schoolteacher, a gas-station attendant, a grocer, a stockbroker, a sea captain, an airplane pilot, a farmer, a professor of English, an artist, and an opera singer. Suppose we instruct them to remain in Chicago two years and then write us a two-thousand-word description of the place, but without mentioning the name of the city. We need only our ordinary knowledge of the facts of daily communication to realize that the result would be so disparate a collection of descriptions it would be hard to believe they all referred to the same city, even though we knew positively that they did.

These various considerations apply triple-force to the serious efforts of very advanced discarnates to convey to us some knowledge of the universe we are all destined to share. It is the same universe. But the educated person will not return a description of it that coincides with that of the illiterate. The schoolteacher will not describe it in just the terms used by the opera singer. The person who was released from his earth body yesterday will be less confident than the individual who entered the new dimension a century ago. The philosopher long resident in the discarnate realm, having much new material for thought, will not offer the same thoughts he distilled from his earth experience. All these differences cannot reasonably be called discrepancies. They are the normal results of varied observers—"peopleness."

Towering about all other difficulties is the problem of vocabulary. Have you ever tried to describe snow and ice to a person who had never been anywhere except near sea level and in the tropics? Such barriers can arise even between temperate-zone people. I remember my frustration in trying to get across the cold, impersonal majesty of an iceberg to someone who had never seen one. Earth is nursery school, our discarnate friends assure us, in trying to describe a universe mostly made up of materials, energies, ideas, customs, resources, and opportunities experienced by earth dwellers only vaguely or not at all.

As one final preliminary to hearing their reports appreciatively, I ask the reader to consider how large a part of his own everyday experience is made up of things he must acknowledge to be real, but which have never come directly to his awareness through any of his conventional five senses. Has anyone ever seen, tasted, felt, or smelled a medium-length electromagnetic wave? Yet we know they are real, that they continually surround us, through the fact that they activate our radio and television sets. Things like gravitation and electricity we know are real, but a good deal of the time we are unaware of them even though they operate continually in and around us. We can describe some of the attributes of these things and even convert them into forms that can be experienced by our senses. But in their essence, vital though they are to our very physical existence, we have been unable to conceive them in their essential nature.

Or take truth itself. How great a difference it makes in our daily lives whether we are dealing with direct truth, or with truth disguised back of misleading appearance! It is among the elements that are real, and all around, but of which we are not fully aware.

This, then, is the first and oft-reiterated message from what we please to call "the Beyond": *there is only one universe.*[2] There have been many instances in my mediumship where grieving survivors, protesting their desolation since the deceased "went away," have been reassured by their lamented discarnates in some variation of the phrase: "But I haven't gone anywhere." There is only one universe, but our normal, earthbound sensory equipment permits us to be aware of only a minute segment of the total spectrum. Just as radio waves and cosmic waves continually pass through our bodies without our knowing, just as tones impinge on our ears too high or low for us to hear, and our eyes cannot see infra or ultra light rays, so the infinite structure of the "many mansions" continually transacts its business around us without our knowing.

Passing to the discarnate world is not going to another place. It is passing to another state of consciousness in which more of the total reality can be comprehended. Dr. Maurice Bucke postulated several conditions of consciousness in which average incarnate human beings habitually live.[3] There is the simple consciousness of the near-animal, aware of immediate sense experience and animal hungers and drives, and little else. There is self-consciousness, wherein the individual is clearly aware of himself as an entity different from all the surrounding universe and interacting with it. There is global consciousness, in which the individual is aware of events on a global scale and senses a responsible personal relationship with them. And finally and most exalted, there is the rare cosmic consciousness, that achieved by great souls, to whom a sense of the meaning of the total universe is revealed. One passes not from one *place* to another, but from one *level of consciousness* to another. This process is evolutionary, is termed the evolution of consciousness, and is an evolutional-educational process some believe to be the central purpose of human life. With this solidly put away—that there is only one universe, and that our progress through it is by a change in levels of consciousness—we are better able to appreciate the intent of some of the messages attempting to describe what we have erroneously been calling "the other side." There is no other side. There are only levels of apprehending a single incomprehensibly vast universe.

Now, how has this universe been described by those observing it as discarnates?

Let us begin with a person only recently passed over,

still full of earth concerns, not yet wholly adjusted to
his new condition, still only partly aware of the possibilities of the new dimension. This is a report of a sitting
given a Pennsylvania resident, Mrs. Edna Davenport, in
October, 1965.

Three months after my husband died I had a sitting
with Arthur Ford. Fletcher came through after Mr.
Ford had gone into trance and said "Hello," and I re-
sponded. He said there was a man here "who knew you
—oh—was with you—a Bud or Buz." He said as Bud
was passing over he called out to you but you did not
answer. "You were dazed." (The nurse said I was in
shock.) Fletcher went on to say that when Bud's
brother, Morrie, reached out his hand to him he knew
where he was. (Bud's brother Morrie had passed over
two years earlier.) Bud said he went over with a clear,
keen mind. He then mentioned some details about our
married life and financial arrangements that were
evidential: nobody could have known about them but
Bud and myself.

Bud (who had been an advertising man) said he had
only one account now, the Spiritual Frontiers Fellowship. He said he didn't want me to wear black (I was
wearing black) because he was not dead. He said he was
happy and active where he was, whereas if he had "lived"
he would have been a semi-invalid. He said, "I have
been with you every night—in fact I am with you more
now than when I was there with you. There are no
closed doors here."

I then asked if it was he who had been ticking and
flickering the light at night. He said he didn't want to
scare me, but wanted me to know he was near. Mr.
Ford started to laugh while in trance, and Fletcher said,
"This man is doing a funny thing. He bows and throws a

kiss." I told Fletcher that was what Bud had done as he left the house each morning. He'd bow and throw a kiss up to the bedroom window where I'd be standing.

Some cases are mixtures of what are often called "trivia" and important factual information about discarnate life. Mrs. Vera Anderson of Montclair, New Jersey has given me a transcript of a sitting held in November, 1967, which contains these two elements. Fletcher told her correctly that she was born in Russia; that her father was killed fighting with the Imperial Cavalry against the Reds; that her mother was a suicide; that her grandmother was called Babushka and her grandfather Peter; that she had five children, all adopted. Then Fletcher, quoting her mother, lets drop some substantial information about "passing over."

We are not sent either to heaven or to hell, we just continue to live. Some of us have to learn many lessons, but as soon as I got out of the body I had no more fear, resentment or hatred, for these are human limitations. I was met by my mother and Alexander (her brother, killed in the revolution). They let me sleep for a while, but not very long. Then I began to function in a perfectly free body. Bless you, I am with you. Know that these sad things are left with the body. Nothing can affect the mind, which is the individualized part of God. The brain can be affected, but it is only a transmitting instrument.

We now progress to a quite different type of sitting. The communicators were all accomplished scientists. All had passed over three to perhaps twenty years before the sitting with Fletcher and me took place in April, 1967. The sitting was recorded by Mrs. A. E. Sharp, another Pennsylvanian. Mrs. Sharp has also provided identifications of the speakers, taken from standard scientific biographical reference works. It is noteworthy here, I think, that the communicators, all having had ample time to become acclimated, have shifted the focus of their interests in several significant ways. They are less absorbed in individual relationships. They are more concerned with matters that might result in benefit or enlightenment for mankind as a whole. They are less preoccupied with individual achievement. They are more concerned with working in groups. Here are Mrs. Sharp's notes.

Discarnate communicators:

Dr. Frederick Simonds Hammett, biochemist, Harvard Ph.D. in biological chemistry, associated with Lankenau Hospital, Philadelphia.

Dr. George Phaler, former head, Department of Radiology, University of Pennsylvania Medical School.

Dr. Hugh I. Evans, former pastor Westminster Church, Dayton, O., Member National Board, Presbyterian Church.

Dr. William Francis Swann (known to his intimates as "Frank"), physicist, former head, Bartol Research Foundation, Franklin Institute, Swarthmore, Pa.

Blank space—indicates living (earth-plane) scientist, name withheld.

Background of April, 1967 sitting: The following came through from Dr. Hammett at a sitting held in May, 1966. After a reference to the Marine Biological Laboratory at Woods Hole, Dr. Hammett said: "The sea is going to be the solution, the growth in the sea."

April, 1967 sitting; excerpts:

Much was said directly by Dr. Hammett, relayed through him by more advanced discarnates. For example:

DR. PHALER: I have been conscious since coming here that nothing over here that is important is done by a single person working alone. When there is a *great* job to be done, a *great task*, they pool their knowledge just as scientists on earth do. No scientist ever develops anything by himself. He only puts together and builds upon the accumulated knowledge and facts of others. Practically every message that is *important* emanates from a *group mind*. You know that when any *great* idea, a great *new* idea is born on earth, it is sort of broadcast so that several people may pick it up at about the same time. We do it that way so that if one isn't interested or fails to stick with it, maybe one of the other people we've been bombarding will do so.

I here interject the observation that the whole history of invention (as reflected in the proceedings of the U.S. Patent Office), of art, and of science is highlighted with examples of important innovations occurring to several people at almost the same time. One of the most striking is connected with Charles Darwin's theory of physical evolution and his explication of it in his *Descent of Man*. Hudson Tuttle, an Ohio farm boy born in 1836, had slightly less than a year of schooling all told. He developed a powerful mediumship while still quite young, and felt that he was being educated by discarnates, among them the great French scientist Lamarck and the celebrated German authority Von Humboldt. Under their tutelage he wrote book after book on history, philosophy, and science. These were of such quality and so widely circulated that Darwin—in his *Descent of Man*—quoted as supporting authority (not knowing the author was an "uneducated" farmer) a book written under discarnate guidance by Tuttle five years earlier. Tuttle remained a

farmer until the end of his days (1910). I continue with
Mrs. Sharp's notes.

DR. PHALER: I didn't know the answer to cancer;
wasted my life working at the wrong angle. But when I
got here I was immediately accepted by Dr. Hammett's
group because they knew my intention was right. Here
you are judged not by an act, or anything you actually
accomplish, but by your intent.

DR. EVANS: There's no reason why a person can't be a
scientist and a spiritual person at the same time. Most
good scientists are spiritual and many are interested in
the psychic.

DR. SWANN: My name is Frank Swann. Tell ————
that I was in research—*pure* research—at the Franklin
Institute. Through my research I was led to a firm belief
in the invisible world and a realization in my own work
that I could dip into the subliminal as a resource . . .
When I became aware of the spiritual power that
blended with material things I was more successful.

The sitting ended with expressions of mutual esteem between the sitter and Fletcher.

My own mediumship, of course, is not the only source
of illustrations for this apparent principle that people grow
in awareness—evolve in level of consciousness—after leaving this plane. Another pair of illustrative sequences can
be drawn from events as far apart as England and California. Sir Oliver Lodge's book *Raymond*[4] ranks among
psychical researchers with the *Proceedings* of the British
Society for Psychical Research as one of the classics. The
Stewart Edward White series reporting the mediumships
of Mrs. White and Mrs. Finley—*The Betty Book*,[5] *The
Unobstructed Universe*[6] and *The Road I Know*[7]—are
similarly well regarded. *Raymond* records the communica-

tions, through various mediums, from Lodge's son, beginning shortly after his death in battle in World War I. The White series is a chronicle of the extraordinarily methodical and well-ordered efforts of very advanced anonymous discarnates to convey to earth-dwellers some basic insights into the nature of the higher realms they will some day inhabit.

In one of his early communications Raymond discusses the predicament of discarnates so recently arrived they have not yet shaken off the habits and appetites of earth life: The medium was Mrs. Leonard; the primary speaker, besides Raymond, is Mrs. Leonard's control, Feda.

He finds it difficult, he says, but he has got so many kind friends helping him . . . He knows that as soon as he is a little more ready he has got a great deal of work to do . . . He seems to know what the work is. First he will have to help at the Front . . . He knows that when they pass on and wake up they still feel a certain fear . . . Some even go on fighting; at least they want to; they don't know they have passed on. So that many are wanted to explain to them and help them and soothe them. They do not know where they are or why they are there. "People think I say I am happy in order to make them happier, but I don't. I have met hundreds of friends. I don't know them all . . . they tell me that they will explain a little later why they are helping me. I feel I have two fathers now. I have my old one and another too—a pro tem. father."

Soon afterwards, F. W. H. Myers spoke from the discarnate world, saying he had "practically adopted" Raymond.

Some time later Raymond, now more assured, tells of his surroundings.

There are men here, and women. I don't think they stand to each other quite the same as they did on the earth plane. But they seem to have the same feeling to each other, with a different expression of it . . . People are sent to the earth plane to have children; they don't have them here. He (says Feda) doesn't want to eat now, but he sees some who do . . . and some want strong drink . . . he has heard of drunkards who want it for months and years . . . (Feda:) He has brought that doggie again . . . He hasn't seen any lions and tigers, but he sees horses, cats, dogs and birds . . . (and still later) . . . He says he's learned so much he couldn't find words to tell you about it through a medium. It's made everything on the earth plane . . . so clear. He often thinks if he could come back, he could fly through life. And, he believes, if only people would go within themselves more, just now and again, they could reach out and get a good deal of what he has learned. But when they want to do things on the earth plane, they don't want to go within themselves because they are afraid of reaching a decision against what they want to do. That is the reason why people can't choose between right and wrong.

One is instantly struck by the difference in tone between the communications of Raymond—at the time a newcomer and in many respects a tyro—and those of "Betty" in trance, as recorded in Stewart Edward White's *The Unobstructed Universe.* After more than two hundred fascinating pages of discourse, through the entranced "Joan" (Mrs. Ruth Finley), of beings—including "Betty," the departed Mrs. White—who could only be described as "very advanced discarnates," White sums up as follows:

Mankind has always had the picture of two entirely

different states of being separated from each other as by a wall—the "on earth" and "in heaven" idea. . . . Betty (and her preceptors) called it the obstructed and unobstructed universes, but she denied the wall between. Her mission in her present divulgence was to knock down that wall. To accomplish this she pointed out, first, that there are not really two universes, but only two aspects of one. We here live in the obstructed aspect, a proposition none of us is likely to deny. Given this fact, the logical deduction would be that she lives in the other, the unobstructed aspect. But that, astonishingly, she asserts, does not follow. On the contrary, says she, she lives in *both* aspects, in the *entire* universe; in the obstructed phase—that tiny percentage of the whole which we of earth inhabit—as well as in the vast and mysterious unobstructed portion she assures us science has glimpsed but of which as yet we know next to nothing. It is one homogeneous universe to her, simply because what are obstructions to us (time, space, "solid" matter) are not obstructions to her.

The evidence accumulates. At this point, after forty years of study, thought, observation, and experience, I hold these truths to be established: Human personality survives bodily death with memory, volition, and capacity for further development. Though the various aspects of consciousness may function independently of one another, one operating without the other's knowledge, there is really no such thing as an absolute unconscious; consciousness can never be "un"; there are only various levels of consciousness, always evolving. There is no such thing as a "supernatural"; the entire universe is governed by natural law, which as yet has only begun to be understood.

The Sun Myung Moon Sittings

10

Sometimes the course of my work seems to recapitulate some of the day. Such a sequence developed around the person of the Korean sage Sun Myung Moon.

Consider some of the ferments currently brewing. Reincarnation, a theme left severely alone by many generations of scholars, is currently having a considerable vogue. Several new books on the subject have appeared. Dr. Ian Stevenson resigned the chairmanship of psychiatry at the University of Virginia to investigate the hundreds of cases reported from the Middle East. "Of the 150 cases I've studied so far," he reports, "I haven't found a single fake."[1] Professors E. E. Bernard of North Carolina State and Charles T. Tart of the University of California are doing studies of out-of-body experiences where people have been shown to be in two places at the same time. An enormous volume of material has appeared in the press on the subject of possible communication with inhabitants of other galaxies. Meditation, in one form or another, has received unprecedented publicity of late. The dissolution and death of old gods and old institutions has also been a theme frequently heard.

Can anyone deny that world revolution, class and border warfare, and civil disturbance have been almost daily in the public eye? Astrology, until recently a dead subject, is booming, with responsible scientists now conceding that there may be "something to" certain of the astrologers' claims.[2] The end-of-an-era theme, the idea of a new start for mankind in the approaching year 2000, cannot have escaped the attention of even the most casual reader. And the idea of ecumenicity, a world agreement among men on principles of living together, has taken hold of most of those, both religious and secular, who dare to look at the world as a whole.

Would it not seem at least a little unusual if *all* these themes were to be explored in some depth in a short sequence of two seances? As I read through the transcript of the tape recordings of the Sun Myung Moon sittings, it seemed to me quite out of the ordinary. Moreover, these sittings provide another opportunity to check the precognition of Fletcher and his co-workers on the "other side." Will the sayings of Mr. Moon achieve the predicted popularity over the next decade or so?[3] Here are significant excerpts from the verbatim record:

Sitting with Arthur Ford, November 2, 1964

Present: Mr. Anthony Brooke of England, for whom the sitting was held; Mr. Walter Voelker, the Rev. W. V. Rauscher, the Rev. Robert Lewis.

FLETCHER (*interpreting for Cyril Arlington, former headmaster of Eton College*): "I got to know Conan Doyle and I couldn't have disagreed with him more completely than I did about spirits. But now I find that it's easier for me to accommodate myself to this method because of the things I remember. It all comes back like the tide. I am very grateful I am able to communicate. I am grateful that you [Anthony Brooke] are taking your place. You know that we used to boast that the British Empire was really organized by boys from Eton. Now it seems to me that in the New Age, in which you are moving, it is not going to be necessary for Eton or anyone else to provide generals and that sort of thing. But we are probably the same brains who helped organize the Kingdom—and the British Empire may be very useful in ushering in the Kingdom of God on earth— and that's far more important. Do you understand?"

ANTHONY BROOKE: I do, indeed.

FLETCHER: And it's God's way. It always starts like the—I don't know—if I had a blackboard I would draw a picture for you. (This man is a very clear thinker, but he is hard to interpret, you see.) I would draw a picture —it looks like a pyramid—like a triangle—on the blackboard. Now at the top there emerges a teacher—it may have been Abraham—it may have been Moses—or it may have been Jesus—or it may have been any one of the great religious leaders. First, there's a solitary figure— then it gradually extends until it spreads out—and that is the symbol. It is from above and has a broad base firmly grounded. And so that has been God's way of making himself known to his people in every generation.

He has with him here a man who, he tells me, was from Denmark. Tells me that he spent over half of his lifetime in Korea. He says that he not only translated the New Testament into the Korean language but also was the first one to make the English-Korean dictionary.

ANTHONY BROOKE: Could you possibly get his name?

FLETCHER: Yes, it's . . . his name is Peter, but it's spelled P-i-e-t-e-r, Pieter Alexander. He came to this country as a child, was educated here, went to Korea around the turn of the century, came back when the invasion took place, and then returned after freedom was declared. And then at a very advanced age he says, "I graduated into this life."

But the point in coming, he says, is that in company with two friends of mine, George Wynn and his wife, who also spent many, many years in that land, I met and talked with this remarkable person who seems to be winning the devotion of a great many people who we had thought were securely anchored in the churches which we had organized. There was something about him that made me feel I was in the presence of a person who was sent by God. I had never been able to quite understand the widespread idea about rebirth or a spirit incarnating again in an earthly body.

And then in our conversation with—they called him Mr. Moon—he gave me what I think is the most logical as well as the most scriptural and probably the true explanation. Spirits on this side progress, but their progression is helped or hindered by things done or undone on the earth plane. And since we find in every human being a quality of God akin to that which we possess, we are able, even though the person is not conscious of it, to work through earthly instruments. And that is the true explanation of the coming of the Holy Spirit.

The whole Spirit individualizes, separates itself into different parts, but never separates itself from the source. But it can blend with a thing that corresponds to its own nature. Practically everyone on the earth plane is in some fashion being used, either as a means of helping someone here to progress, or to help someone on the earth plane to speak the Word or do the thing that is necessary. It is a sort of universal power, like electric current.

Here you have a great big bulb, maybe 100 watts, and there is a 60-watt—then there is a small one—then there are little tiny ones. Each one of these represents a degree of culture or civilization on the earth, and each one reflects as much of the universal current as that particular bulb is able to incorporate and make manifest. And Mr. Moon told me that he did not believe that reincarnation was true or was a fact, in the sense that a spirit entered into and became completely bound up in the physical organism of another person.

God does individualize in that person but nearly every person is carrying around what the psychotherapist or the psychiatrist would say is an obsession—but Mr. Moon insists that it is an incarnation. It may last for a while or it may be for a lifetime. It all depends upon the dedication of the person and the task that is to be accomplished.

Then there is a highly sensitized person, and he becomes the vehicle which is used either permanently or periodically by a spirit from high planes. He takes on some of the personality and some of the characteristics of that spirit until he begins to act like it. And then his own consciousness absorbs the knowledge which is passing through him in some cases: "I am Moses," or I am this, or I am that, and to some extent he may be. But that is what is meant by the coming of the Spirit of Truth. It is, and he made it clear to me that the more highly evolved a person becomes spiritually the more impersonal he becomes in the sense that, like St. Paul said, "I died that Christ may live"—and then at another time he said, "I die daily."

And Mr. Moon made it clear that every man who is seeking spiritual growth or understanding has to die— because in dying it means you are pushing—(not physical death, that's of no moment whatever)—your selfishness, your desires, your egocentric being is daily pushed further and further away from the center of your being so that the spiritual impulse that seeks to express itself through you can become manifest.

And there is no happiness that can transcend the happiness of death—the death of selfish interest, personal self-centered desires, and all those things which are causing man to be, even while in the body, earth-bound more truly than he could be even when he is free from the physical body. That is true happiness—to become part of the Universal Mind and Heart and to express it.

And so a person may very well say, "I know I have lived before," because he is acting under the guidance of a person who has lived on earth and who now lives through him. And if you read your Bible with understanding, you will know that "the end of the age" not "the end of the earth" (for there will be no physical destruction of the age—a type of civilization) will ultimately result in a supracivilization, which may be what you mean by the Kingdom of God.

But at the end of the age from which you are just emerging you enter a New Age. It was said that there would be many false Christs and many people would claim to be what they were not—and they would lead the people astray in many directions. And those are the people who are just as real as the rest of us, but who have for some reason refused to accept the spiritual heritage which they had a right to claim.

Mr. Moon says a person—a psychic or a medium who may be controlled by an entity who hasn't been here very long and who probably is still expressing and trying to validate some of the things that she believed while on earth—may look at you and become aware of a personality that is more than you are at this moment—at this particular hour of your life. She may get the idea that she is dealing with another incarnation. There is no reincarnation in the sense that there is a law which drives people back over and over again, but there is a law of correspondence. And when Jesus said, "It is necessary that I go, because if I (and the word 'I' as he used it meant 'I' the limited ego, which you know as your friend Jesus)—if I do not go the Spirit of Truth cannot come." In other words, he knew that he could only manifest in the highest and truest sense and speak the final truth, the spiritual truth, when he was no longer handicapped by personality—when he was no longer limited to the recognition on the part of his friends that he was just Jesus of Nazareth.

They could not always know that there was something more than the carpenter's son. There was something using him. And that is what I meant when I said, "The things that I do you could do, because I will send the Whole Spirit—the Spirit out from the top—until it envelops and involves all those who are ready to receive it." And that was the only time I ever really understood the Oriental preoccupation with the idea of rebirth. Rebirth is a spiritual thing. The spirit uses physical instruments, but is not limited to them.

Pieter Alexander says, "George Wynn was with me and Lillian Wynn was with me when we met him. Because I was fluent in the language and different dialects I was able to understand what he meant. I did not mean to stay so long, but I wanted to tell you that because I saw these young clergymen here."

ANTHONY BROOKE: Could you say anything about the significance of Mr. Moon in relation to any other individual in the flesh today?

FLETCHER: You mean in interpersonal relationships?

ANTHONY BROOKE: What can you tell us about Sun Myung Moon?

FLETCHER: His mission is as a teacher, a revealer. At the end of an age always there must be a few, sometimes

even one, who will become the voice of this Intelligence
—Creative Mind—which you call God. His relationship
is to the rest of the world what that of many have been
in the past. Abraham spoke and became the voice of God
for a tribe. Moses spoke and became the voice of God
for a nation. Jesus spoke and became the voice of
God for the whole world. But the Anointed One cannot
die—God cannot die. And the effort that is necessary
now and the divine purpose for which Mr. Moon (is)
brought into your consciousness is simply stated in this
way, "It is necessary (he is the voice of inspiration,
guidance) to restore to mankind an understanding of
his full nature and his relationship to God."

And out of the shambles of a crumbling civilization
and above the cries of distress that you hear in every
part of your world today, there is a plan slowly and
definitely unfolding to restore man to the state of
perfection which is necessary if he is to live happily and
handle wisely the instruments that materialistic science
has wrested from this mysterious and growing universe.

Restoration not of anything of the past simply because it belongs to the past, but restoration of the basic
truths out of which all civilizations and all religions have
grown.

There have been many and each one of them has been
solitary until he has touched and inspired others—and
gradually the pyramid spread out. He is not the first, nor
the last. But for the present moment he is, in my estima-
tion, a most important spiritual light that shines in the
darkness of your confused world. . . .

And he has the rare quality of projecting himself,
which isn't a miracle really. It's simply an employment
of techniques which swamis, yogis, and holy men have
known and which the saints have known for projection
until you become real and visible to your devotees or

people whom you need in order to further the kingdom. Mr. Moon in deep meditation can project himself and be seen just as Jesus has been able to project himself and be seen by the saints. This is one of the marks of the messiahs always.

WALTER VOELKER: What can we ourselves do to help?

FLETCHER: Hear the word and do not allow tradition to blind you to revelation. You must remember that every person that comes with revelation that threatens the selfish interests of people entrenched in anything on earth is going to be persecuted. But we know here that when a person burns another at the stake, or crucifies him or hangs him, it is because unconsciously the spirit within him is telling him that the person he is crucifying is right. But he cannot afford to admit *that* because he has accepted the persecutor—the hangman—the crucifier—as maintaining traditional beliefs.

And so whenever you find anyone persecuting another person you know that the one who is persecuting is doing it in order to keep himself from admitting the truth. And he is killing the one who threatens his security, because the inquisitor is always unsure. He is guilty and his insecurity drives him to a frenzy—that is why you have such hatred, such strife on earth today. People in vast numbers are clinging to things which they no longer believe. But they have not been willing to listen. Therefore, in their ignorance, they destroy the secure person who threatens their security. That is why the person who is crucified is always calm and even happy in the hour of his martyrdom. He is sure.

WALTER VOELKER: How can we reach others and bring this to their attention?

FLETCHER: I know of no way except individuals who experience God in some form—who have had the courage to look at what they are and what they have and what they believe through the lens of revelation and inspiration—then speak.

The Church is undergoing a transformation because it is inevitable at this particular point in history—the beginning of a New Age and the end of an old one. Even the Church with its holy traditions has to bring Christ down from the stained-glass window—take him from the altar—put him in the hearts of men—let him walk the streets.

And the Christ always has as a symbol of his authority the child—and when the Christ was worshiped as a child, he was not worshiped by those in authority—it was by those who had lived and looked into the heavens and read the course of man.

Mr. Moon reminded me that in the Book of Revelation there is a picture of the New Jerusalem, the Holy City, coming down out of the heavens. And there was a door on the east and a door on the south, a door on the north and a door on the west—and when the teacher comes, he always has to come through the eastern gate. In the Holy City of Jerusalem there is an eastern gate long since sealed and blocked. It will never be opened until the new teacher comes.

From the *east* comes mysticism—a willingness to be absorbed in God—God is not something apart—he is something within. From the *south* comes all the beauty, the ritual—these things which adorn and make beautiful the message. From the *north* came rational thought—clear thinking—reformation—and change. From the *west* came the critical, scientific analysis.

And now in the New Age, it is an age of orchestration—of a symphony—of unity. And the New Teacher will be neither Christian, Buddhist, Moslem, or anything else. The Holy Spirit speaks in universal terms—and God will no longer be fragmented. God will be the one God—who sent forth his Son not once but many times.

ANTHONY BROOKE: At this point can you say something about the spirit that is appearing in England that calls himself Truth and who has been seen by some people in solid form?

FLETCHER: That's Mr. Moon's projection—a form of apparition—the projection of the Spirit of Truth—who expresses himself through Mr. Moon. In other words, in the language of the occult mystery schools, it's the astral or spiritual body of Mr. Moon projected and seen by those who are ready for it. You must remember that when Jesus of Galilee was crucified and buried—when he came back in his spiritual body he was seen only by those who had known him and whom he wanted to see him. Those who were not prepared did not see him. But then he spoke—on the Bay of Galilee he broke through all national boundaries and all tribal taboos—and every man heard the message in his own way. In other words, he became the Holy Spirit—the Whole Spirit—speaking no longer only to Jews—but speaking to everyone from the then known world. It's always the method of. . . .

ANTHONY BROOKE: Can you say how near we are to such a breakthrough of universal truth?

FLETCHER: You are in the process now. But before Jesus became manifest there were people who had been prepared—John the Baptist came—prepared. But the world has grown and multiplied—the means of communication have become simpler and easier. It takes not one man in a little country to be a John the Baptist, but many men in many countries to herald the coming.

Sitting with Arthur Ford, March 18, 1965, 3:30 P.M.

Present: Mr. Sun Myung Moon, for whom the sitting was held; Col. Bo Hi Pak, former attaché of the Korean Embassy; Miss Kim, interpreter for Sun Myung Moon,

Mr. Walter Voelker, the Rev. W. V. Rauscher, the Rev. Robert Lewis, and a group of Mr. Moon's friends from Korea, Japan, the United States, and other places.

ARTHUR FORD: I studied with Yogananda. He used the word "detachment," which means we completely detach from the objective. There's a larger mind. You never know what will happen. What happens, happens because of the people who are here.

When Fletcher comes, I am totally unconscious. That proves its complete detachment. I can't remember anything. It isn't merely hypnosis. Fletcher is using words through me, using my voice. Naturally, they don't use words over there. Words are physical sounds. He has to interpret thoughts and ideas, that sort of thing, and put them into words. And, of course, it's as St. Paul says, when he went up into the Third Heaven, he saw things and heard things which are unutterable. It's something you feel.

When Fletcher comes, we'll do the best we can. You can ask any questions you want, he'll tell you who's there. He will establish identities.

I haven't used this handkerchief since you were here before.

COL. PAK: I remember that handkerchief.

ARTHUR FORD: I do this, because it's easier to go to sleep.

(*At this point Arthur Ford went into trance.*)

FLETCHER: It is not easy for me to get down to the level of Ford. Great power in the form of light—if you were to see the light that surrounds you—most of you would be blinded by it. I am conscious that there are people here who are spiritually more advanced than some here and certainly more advanced than I am, though I have been here nearly fifty years. Time does not guarantee spirituality, nor does it necessarily suggest growth.

In another setting I would insist that my instrument and the rest of you should take off your shoes. But spiritually you can create the humility that will enable you to *know* that you are in the presence of Truth—Incarnate and Discarnate.

I am surrounded by people who are not the kind of people I usually interpret for. A man who is here speaks —he says he is grateful for the opportunity—he has something, somehow, to do with some of you. He gives the name of Kousik. It's K. K.—Kim Kousik. He shows me a paper which seems to bear his name. I read his name. I see the man. The paper I cannot read . . .

It seems to me that there is one man here who was here before. Your name is Colonel or something. You know who Kousik is?

COL. PAK: Yes, Kim Kousik was one of the political statesmen in Korea.

FLETCHER: He shows me a document which seems to have significance as if his name were on it. He says he regrets very much that Lee Wan Tong is not with you. Tong Wan Lee. Do you know who that is?

COL. PAK: Foreign Minister of Korean Government.

FLETCHER: You have seen him lately?

COL. PAK: Yes, I saw him two days ago.

FLETCHER: Tell him that he did well to come here. . . . This is the end of an age, and the battle that is raging is really Armageddon. It's a battle between the selfish, brutal men who do not think in terms of God—or things which are associated with that word—against those peoples who will be the harbingers of the New Age. You are now in the New Age—and old things are being destroyed—and new things—which are eternal but which are new only because mankind has now reached the point where it is able to recognize them and use them.

And some of you in this room, some of you who come from other lands and some of you who are native to this land belong in the vanguard of the New Age. And there is a gentleman in the room who is one of those who will be used for the restoration of spiritual principles and truths which are eternal, but which have been lost because of the stupidity and the greed of men. You can safely follow him, because nothing that is in the universe that is real is ever destroyed—it changes form.

But there are many things in the minds and consciousness of men which are distortions of Truth and approximations of Truth and they are many times superstitions which have been grafted upon Truth. They do not destroy, but they present Truth in such a manner that it does not have significance or meaning to the people who are looking for salvation—which means only a restoration of the eternal affinity between the Creator and his creations. I don't know what they're talking about, but that's what he says.

COL. PAK: Could you ask him in connection with the New Age, more specifically, the mission of Our Leader here today?

FLETCHER: He is one of those who will be the human instrument through whom the World Teacher will be able to speak. And he was chosen because the New Age can be ushered in only through the eastern gate of the City of God—and that gate has been sealed since Jesus was crucified. It cannot be opened until the New Age in which you are now entering and which you are in. When the teacher comes there would be a people ready for him.

The Jesus of Galilee will not return—it is not necessary. The Christ who manifested through him is the Eternal —he will manifest again. He has never ceased to speak to

men but the time has come when, in the New Age, the
veil which has been drawn between your plane and the
World of Spirit will be pushed aside and those who have
been freed from physical bondage will be able to speak
and use and guide and teach the peoples of earth. That
is being brought into manifestation everywhere.

But the important thing to remember is that when
God wants to make a revelation (he has always done so
and always will) he has to choose a human instrument,
who, through some circumstances or conditions, has been
brought to the point of sensitiveness and spiritual perception so that *he* can, in his own person, accept this
ancient light of wisdom—and through him it will filter
down to others, probably no less dedicated, but, in truth,
less gifted.

It is like a pyramid. At the peak stands the Teacher,
the Leader, the Chosen One and under him, gradually
there begins to build a foundation. The truth flows down,
and as it flows down it flows outward until it touches
every corner of the earth. But it always starts with one
man—and others are touched.

The Holy Spirit has not been quiet—and he has not
been inactive. But there come periodically in the history
of the race moments when the Holy Spirit has to individualize almost completely in some person—who becomes
the instrument who will enable others to catch the Spirit
and see the Spirit, and know the Spirit. And so they
go in all directions, never separated from the source, but
always individualized. . . .

Sun Myung Moon is the one I have been talking about.
I have been speaking for a group of people here. This
group seems to surround him. And the power that flows
through him, the intelligence, is not just one—it is a
great group of people. And they seem all to draw
their inspiration and their knowledge from One Source

—and then they seem to pour it symbolically into a pool and in some strange symbolical way that pool becomes Sun Myung Moon.

As if All Experience—All Knowledge—All Spiritual Truth has always existed. It has been revealed at different times—through different people. But the one who reveals is concerned only that he speaks Truth and those who are ready and capable of accepting Truth or perceiving Truth—they carry the message on. The revelators seldom live to see their revelations widely accepted. But they do always draw to them—and leave behind them—a group who continue the revelation.

WALTER VOELKER: May I ask a question, Fletcher? For persons like me, familiar with the teachings of Jesus and to whom the Divine Principles seem strange, can anyone tell the relationship between the "teachings of Jesus" and the "messages of Sun Myung Moon" so that I will not be confused?

FLETCHER: I will have to speak for the people here. Truth never contradicts itself. Quite often what you call the teachings of Jesus may be—they often are—interpretations which men have made, and about which men have builded institutions. You cannot, in your age, rely upon any ancient formula or any ancient definitions of God or man. The other religions developed dogmas and doctrines about both man and God. And when they declared them, science challenged them—and then chaos, confusion, set in.

In the age in which you are living, all the debris that has accumulated around Truth must be brushed aside, for all Truths become loaded with ideas, organizations, which grow up in the heart of devout people, but which have no relation really to the Truth itself. And so today you live in a time when men know a great many facts, but they haven't learned how to identify these facts—this data—with ideals. And a scientific knowledge without philosophical reflection can result in emptiness. And that is what you face.

You cannot limit God. And you cannot limit the possibilities of man, because man has within him individualized part of the God, of the Infinite. But if you try to build a life, a philosophy, or a religion only on those facts which you are able to perceive through your senses—and if you rely only upon sensory perception and experience, you will not find the Truth.

Scientific facts are important, but in themselves they tell you nothing. Scientific facts become meaningful only when they are used against a vast background of ideas and ideals. Therefore, what I am saying is that the Basic Truths are that *God is* and that *man is his creation* —and being God's creation began as a perfect being but through environmental conditions and through ignorance and—sometimes because of instinctual promptings which overpowered his divinity—man has lost that perfection which he had as a creature of God. And man himself has created a dual universe.

There was no Evil in God's creation; there is no Evil in the Mind of God. But man through his own choice —and because he has yielded to the instinctual urges which are a heritage of his animal ancestry as a physical vehicle—has created a dual universe. And the purpose of the New Age is to restore that perfection, which can only be realized when man becomes completely God-centered and then into the social processes brings the qualities of justice and love and brotherhood, which are the attributes of the spiritual concept of God. Then you will demolish a dual universe.

And Satan, which is only the ancient word for Eternal Hatred, will be destroyed—because where there is love, there can be no hate, and that is what the prophets and

Jesus himself prophesied—"at the end of the age" not "the end of the world"—and you have ended that age and are entering *now* an age in which you will be compelled to subjugate those people who would destroy you. And you will be compelled to end the Battle of Armageddon. But it will be a victory in which all the selfish nationalism, the creeds, the hates that grow out of these things will be ended. It will not be finished in your lifetime, but your lifetime is not limited to this little expression through your physical bodies. You will still be a part of the chosen; you will still be a part of those who will be influencing and guiding and throwing light on the path of those who will build the Kingdom of God on earth.

You must not fall victim to the false idea that there is any such thing as a final truth once and for all delivered. Truth is a living, vibrant thing, because truth stems from God, and there is no conclusion; there is no goal except that ever expanding goal of God. But, in some strange way, the divine economy demands that every so often some man take upon himself a larger share of God and thus become the Voice of Truth. It has always been so and always will be so, and there will always be those who can be used.

God has no voice save the voice that is given to him by people who have risen to the point where they can comprehend and then extend his ideas. . . .

Miss Kim: Do you mean the Christ of 2,000 years ago?

Fletcher: There was no Christ 2,000 years ago—there was a *man* 2,000 years ago through whom the Anointed One was able to manifest. The man died—Christ lived—and, as the Holy Spirit, has been helping. You must remember that, when this man said, "I will be with you until the end of the age," it was not the Galilean speaking, it was the Incarnate Christ. . . .

MISS KIM: Will there be many leaders in the New Age?

FLETCHER: Even if there is a Christ he had to choose the twelve, and they, in turn, touched the lives of others. Because the message could not have been given if it had been limited to one man, to one race, to one group. But always, as this man said, it has to start with one man—and always the revelation is founded upon the truth *once* revealed, but it is added to, and expressed in terms not of yesterday, but of the future. . . . There must always be someone who can accept the responsibility of passing the truth on.

COL. PAK: You are speaking of New Revelation: that means you are speaking of—you refer to—the Divine Principles brought by Sun Myung Moon?

FLETCHER: That's a part of it, yes, but even Sun Myung Moon has not exhausted the possibilities of the Divine Mind. He is, and as long as he lives will continue to be, a channel for revelation. The channel never ceases to flow; the fountain never dries up. . . . Always it will be the Spirit of Truth—who is not limited in any direction by either a group, a man, or anyone else—he uses one man—or he may use a million men, but he is never limited.

The Spirit of Truth, like the sun, will light the whole world.

MISS KIM: Do you know that there should be one true father and mother—true parents for the New Age?

FLETCHER: The Divine Mind or the Concept of God has—as a creative principle—God has within himself all the faculties or the qualities of both the male and the female. There can be no creative expression, there can be no life without these two qualities—the male and the female. So God is neither man nor woman. He sums up within himself all things. . . . There's a man who comes here, and he says that he wishes to speak. He seems to have known some of you. He gives the name of John Gilmer. He says he died in Seoul. Some of you from there? Seoul? John Gilmer, he says he was there and he knew and met some of you there. He was with the United Nations on some kind of an economic survey. And he says he was with Albert Wedemeyer.

COL. PAK: Yes, General Wedemeyer. . . . I knew his name.

FLETCHER: He says that he comes because he died just recently, almost within days or hours, in Seoul, this John Gilmer. He says that he wants to tell you that there are in your land great possibilities, and they must be utilized. You must not forget that to feed the hungry, clothe the naked, and heal the sick—all these things are as spiritual as it is to pray or to worship God. And you must translate your spiritual truth into those things which make for justice and for peace and for happiness—so that men can know God—because you cannot talk about God to men who are starving unless you present God in the form of bread. You cannot interest men in God if they are naked unless you can clothe them and keep them warm. And a man who is sick because of deprivation and unhappy conditions will not listen about God unless you help to relieve those conditions—then you have found God in action. . . . And now you enter a New Age—you have to live through Armageddon—you have to live through the death struggle of those who seek to perpetuate the old days—but you will emerge into the Light. . . . There is someone here who's been talking, several, but one who is talking in light, someone who gives the name Kim Koo.

COL. PAK: Yes, a martyred patriot in Korea.

FLETCHER: I died that they might find freedom. Our

land has never known the freedom even to worship God as our hearts told us to. We were always having foreign religious ideas imposed upon us. Now we have freedom —and so when that freedom was ours, Sun Myung Moon was used by the Holy Spirit, and is used by the Holy Spirit, and will be used by the Holy Spirit. Translate the things he tells you into activities that lift poverty and hunger and hate.

I can assure you that there will be no war that will destroy Korea or the world—even Satan is wise enough to know when he must retreat. Error cannot live where the light of truth is to be found.

WALTER VOELKER: What advice does he have for us?

FLETCHER: This man has a message—this *man* has no message—but the Holy Spirit, the Spirit of Truth, can speak through Moon more clearly—more completely— than he is able to speak through any one individual today. It may take a long time for his truth to be realized in the hearts of men. But even the Christ had to have his John the Baptist to herald him—and then, after he came, he had to gather around him a group—and after his death that group bore witness—and it's a long time.

There is but one God. There is but one Christ. He may wear different names, because men speak different tongues, but there is but *one God, one Christ, one Spirit of Truth.* Whenever that Spirit of Truth becomes vocal, you are wise to listen.

Remember to make the distinction between the Spirit of Truth, which is the Christ, and any individual with a human name. That name may become historically associated with the Spirit of Truth. The Spirit of Truth didn't begin with any man—it ends with no man—it uses men. Right now it is using in a very remarkable way the man who is in your presence.

COL. PAK: May I ask you one thing? Our leader, Sun

Myung Moon is a prince of the New Age. We feel that he has completed national scale restoration. Now his work is going on in the world on a universal scale. How will the world accept him? In his lifetime how much will the world be changed?

FLETCHER: It was Kim Koo, who came because he said "even in effecting political and national and economic freedom we have to use people." . . .

You have reached a point—the world has reached a point—where a person can speak in terms of principles. And remember that principles are flexible and are capable of being applied individually. They are adaptable to culture and to wisdom. A principle is the reality behind law. Most of you are no longer spiritually under law. Law is a fixed and sometimes cruel and heartless and ruthless thing. You have grown spiritually to the point where you live on principle, which is the truth behind law. Primitive peoples still need the law. God is able to make himself understood in terms and in manner that is understood—and that is adapted to the culture in which it is sprinkled. Strange thing. Does the name Indra mean anything?

COL. PAK: It could be a Korean woman's name.

FLETCHER: Whoever this woman is, she says something about some kind of a memorial—it looks like it's a symbol—a picture of what will grow and it is no mere accident that it happened in Pusan. A memorial to people of all nations. And that memorial was consecrated and dedicated by representatives of every one of the world religions who came together on the soil of Korea to build a memorial, not to the people of one race—one religion. And Kim Koo says it is no accident that on the 21st of last August representatives of every race and every religion gathered in Pusan to build some kind of a sacred something which is a symbol of what will grow out and spread over the world—and it has something to do with some kind of a memorial. It was established just a few days after this holy 15th of August. What's the 15th of August?

COL. PAK: The 15th of August is the day we celebrate the birth of freedom, the Independence Day of Korea.

WALTER VOELKER: May I ask a question, Fletcher? Do we have within ourselves a guide that tells us what is God's will? Or do we take in an authoritarian way the opinion or statement of another, such as Sun Myung Moon, without qualifications?

FLETCHER: The Spirit speaks to spirit and every one of you has within you something—an individualized part of that whole which you call God. Truth may flow to everyone, it is not limited to any one man. Always there are illumined souls who can become teachers, guides, and through whom the truth can flow more fully. It did through Christ—it did through Buddha—it did through others. But none of these people—and neither does Mr. Moon himself—claim to be God—he only claims, like Jesus and the others, to be an instrument through whom the Spirit of Truth is able to speak. And when the Spirit of Truth speaks through any man, no matter who it is, listen. When he speaks more fully, listen more carefully. . . .

MISS KIM: Should the Christians all over the world continue to follow Jesus of Nazareth or the Divine Principles?

FLETCHER: The Christians all over the world have never followed Jesus of Nazareth as a *man*—they have only followed Christ who was incarnate for a little while in the person of Jesus—you must make the distinction. It is not going to be possible for anyone to suddenly sweep all the religious peoples of the world into one group. It is a process of education into a part of the world where

Christ was not known, and where his teachings were presented very poorly by those who claimed to represent him.

It was necessary that Mr. Moon should come. God had to have some man through whom the Spirit of Truth could speak, because the missionaries were not speaking in the same language—they were all presenting a different picture. There is but one Spirit of Truth. And so the distortions of men have always made it necessary for someone to become the revelator. . . .

COL. PAK: Could you give me some forecast of our leader's work, the teaching and educational process of of this new truth, in the United States?

FLETCHER: First of all, he must be willing to listen, to speak, and then have his words translated—and they will be translated into many languages. But you cannot expect the message to be accepted immediately by vast numbers of people—only those who are ready and who are willing to listen and to whom this particular message seems to be right and meaningful. That is the way that all the world teachers have had to go. And remember one thing only, that if it is of God, it cannot fail. And it is of God.

But Mr. Moon is just one in a long line of people who have been used as revelators—he is not the last—he is not the first—but in this hour, he is being used in a great way. And his message will be heard. Does that answer your question?

This is the thing to remember (and with this I must go—the power is waning)—this is the thing I would leave with you—that any man who has the good fortune to find a teacher of truth, and that teacher speaks to his need and to his heart, that man is under a divine compulsion to *share* his joy and his knowledge, and, if possible, lead others so that each may stand in the presence of his teacher—and enter into an experience of his own.

But never make the mistake of associating the truth which flows from any man, through any man, of identifying it completely with that man. The Spirit of Truth uses men. It is not a man.

WALTER VOELKER: Quick question, Fletcher, please. What is my greatest weakness? What is the weakness that you see in other persons like us here?

FLETCHER: I see just what we all see here—a great confusion in the minds of men everywhere—because ancient formalism, traditions are being struck down in the light of new knowledge. You have almost reached the point—world-wide as men, incarnate men—where you seem to *know* everything, *understand* nothing.

Gather your data, gather you knowledge, listen to your teachers. But remember there's always a vast dimension of spiritual power and truth, and until you are able to become aware of that, all the knowledge, all the facts, all the data mean nothing, because it doesn't cohere. God is the coherent—the integrative—the symphonic power in the universe. . . . I have been speaking for a group of people. Now, there's just one man who says he wants to speak to these young clergymen. He also wants to speak to Col. Pak. Did you attend the war crimes trials?

COL. PAK: Yes, during the war.

FLETCHER: There's a man here who says he knows some of the people that know these young clergymen. He says that he was appointed to defend Tojo as a war criminal of Japan. This man says, "I am an American and it is interesting that I used to go to the Episcopal church in Paoli. I was with the Army—with MacArthur and I was appointed, because I was an advocate, to defend Tojo. I lost the case, and I rather hoped I would—I did not care about winning the case." And he said, "Just a little while ago, I was killed by a train in Paoli, recently. My name is George Bluitt. I was in Korea."

And this man, John Gilmer, says, "Things will be better."

COL. PAK: When he said things will be better—things are looking better—was he speaking of our movement?

FLETCHER: Your movement and the world generally —because you are living through the death agony of an old order. It takes time for the New Age to discard the debris, the accumulated stupidities of the order—they go and they are going. . . . anyway, he has confirmed some of my theories that there is a possibility—that people on other planets are trying to communicate on a megacycle of about—I think he said—900.

VOELKER: Right.

FLETCHER: So . . . if these faint and unusual things that he picked up are true, it would take nearly 500 years as you reckon time on earth for a message to reach him from inhabited planets. But I was convinced, and I think now it must have been a moment of illumination, that there is life on other planets. They are older than ours, and they are eagerly exploring their kind of outer space.

There is a sort of unconscious, not unconscious, but there's a sort of spiritual guidance that is helping to coordinate the efforts of interplanetary communications. That's going to be a part of the New Age. And it isn't any mere accident. You remember this. This man Nicholi is a great astronomer, and it's no accident that the dominant planet in the constellation which now controls and will determine the destiny of the earth planet— the dominant planet was named Uranus. Without that symbol you would not have the propulsion necessary to accomplish this thing.

Give my love and regards to Alding, and you can assure him that there will be no dropping of nuclear bombs in the foreseeable future—probably never. Goodbye."

ALL: Goodbye, Fletcher. God bless you.

It may be noted that *Time* magazine for November 6, 1964 (p. 38), published the following, under the title, "Mystery from Way Out":

One of those far-out fantasies that have long been a staple of science fiction is now a serious subject for scientific discussion—with the Russians taking it to new extremes. Two unusual radio "stars," wrote Astronomer Nicolai S. Kardashev in the *Astronomical Journal* of the Soviet Academy of Sciences, may be "supercivilizations" deep in space, calling attention to themselves by transmitting vast amounts of energy on peculiar, and therefore conspicuous, radio frequencies.

. . . The most remarkable thing about them is the radio energy they emit: it is strongest at about 900 megacycles. This frequency, says Kardashev, is the best for long-distance space communication. . . .

Developing Latent Psychic Ability

11

The preceding chapters contain several references to the fact that everybody has some psychic ability. Like every other human capacity—running, dancing, lifting heavy weights, spelling, or doing sums—this ability may be developed to high degree or allowed to atrophy. Some will be discovered to possess unusual gifts, some will turn out to be mediocre. Some of my readers want to develop whatever psychic ability they have; others, preoccupied with matters they find more pressing, don't. This chapter is intended for those who do.

People who want to develop their latent psychic abilities generally fall into one of three classes. In the first class I would include all those who seek a closer relationship with the ultimate Power from whom all things emanate. This is called by various names, according to one's tradition. People grounded in one of the major religions will call it God. Those adhering to ethical agnostic views may refer to the same Power as Life Force, Cosmic Mind, or Prime Mover. Because of my own conditioning I use, for the most part, a candidly Christian terminology. This need not prevent adherents of other concepts from sharing my central experience—parallel expressions of the same truth can be found in all of the redemptive traditions.

The second category of potential psychic devotees is made up of those who have no spiritual aspirations, but who are curious, in a casual or even scientific way, about their abilities in this fascinating field. These people are herewith warned that, unless they remain open-minded about the possibility of being led into deeper waters, and are receptive to such leading, their experience will almost certainly turn out to be a blind alley.

The third category consists of people who covet psychic potency out of lust for personal power, prestige, profit, or sensual gratification. To these last my advice is unequivocal: either develop higher motivation or drop the whole business at once. The consequence of deliberate misuse of these abilities can be disastrous.

I ask, first, a scientific approach.

The developing scientist first learns the tradition of his specialty. From this he learns that, though many of the techniques he will use are new, some have changed but little from the very beginning of his particular discipline. Oxygen is today being produced for laboratory demonstration exactly as it was by Scheele and Priestley two centuries ago. Surveyors today use principles propounded by Euclid in 300 B.C. So it is with psychic science: the way has been well charted by those who have gone before.

"In the very process of the mystical approach," says the contemporary British thinker Paul L. Higgins, "there are very often psychic phenomena. Most of the great mystics demonstrated powers we identify as psychic and had experiences which embraced manifestations generally considered paranormal or extrasensory. . . . The great mystics have warned against seeking simply psychic experiences;

these great souls have again and again stressed the spiritual life. . . ."[1]

To establish our mental set, we can do no better than to catch something of the mood of Phillips Brooks when he said, "There is nothing more striking in the Bible than the calm, familiar way with which from end to end it assumes the present existence of a world of spiritual beings always close to and acting upon this world of flesh and blood. . . . There is no reserve, no vagueness that would leave a chance for the whole system to be explained away into dreams and metaphors. The spiritual world, with all its multitudinous existence, is just as real as the crowded cities and fragrant fields and loud battlegrounds of the visible. . . ."

A striking example of what Brooks means is found in St. Paul. A powerful psychic himself, Paul observed these abilities in others and carefully listed them. It is scientifically noteworthy, I think, that his enumeration of these gifts has never been added to or subtracted from. Paul's list appears in his first letter to the Corinthians, the twelfth and thirteenth chapters: "About gifts of the Spirit, there are some things of which I do not wish you to remain ignorant. . . . In each of us the Spirit is manifested in one particular way, for some useful purpose. One man, through the Spirit, can put the deepest knowledge into words. Another, by the same Spirit, is granted faith; another, by the one Spirit, gifts of healing, and another miraculous powers; another has the gift of prophecy, and another the ability to distinguish true spirits from false; yet another has the gift of ecstatic utterance of different kinds, and another the ability to intrepret it. . . . And now I will show you the best way of all. . . . love. . . . There is nothing love cannot face; there is no limit to its faith, its hope, and its endurance. . . . When I was a child, my speech, my outlook, and my thoughts were all childish" (Freudian psychoanalysis). "When I grew up I had finished with childish things" (client-centered therapy). "Now we see only puzzling reflections in a mirror" (frustrated communication), "but then we shall see face to face. My knowledge now is partial; then it will be whole, like God's knowledge of me. In a word, there are three things that last forever" (as special psychic gifts do not): "faith, hope and love; but the greatest of them all is love."[2] Modern parapsychology has found nothing to add to these categories of psychic gifts. If one does develop psychic ability, it is certain to be one or another of these.

The prominent American clergyman Dr. Wickizer likes to use an anecdote from Maeterlinck as a pointer to those embarking on inward exploration. A small community clustered about a lighthouse on a remote and dangerous shore was put in dire straits when the supply ship was late. Because he loved his neighbors the lighthouse keeper began sharing his surplus oil. Finally it was gone, and the beacon failed to burn that night. Lacking its guidance, the supply ship went on the rocks and its crew and supplies were lost. "Don't give away all your oil," advises Maeterlinck, "let your gift be the flame." Dr. Wickizer observes that "in our activism we have been too much driven by external affairs to neglect the cultivation of our inner resources."

The deliberate cultivation of psychic ability certainly does not call for abandonment of objective activity. It only suggests that the inner and the outer worlds be brought more appropriately into balance. Dr. Gene E. Bartlett brought these two worlds into relationship when he remarked: "God spoke to Moses from a burning bush; He may speak to us in a burning issue." The inner insight, in other words, must come first. It may then be followed by outward activity in its propagation.

Two words intrude themselves at the very beginning of

any effort to grasp the inward life, and we may as well deal with them now. One is "prayer." The other is "meditation." These are frankly devotional words. To one who detests the sanctimonious and is suspicious of the man who claims to know all about God, such words can be upsetting. What, exactly, is "prayer"? In a parapsychological context, it is usually defined as a special form of telepathic communication, directed to involve the intended receiver more or less as radio waves are reflected by the ionosphere to sets tuned to receive them.

"Meditate"—what does *that* mean? Whatever else it may mean, all experienced authorities agree that it begins by being alone and being quiet—*really* alone, and really quiet. Quiet not just in the ears, but deep in the body, deep in the mind, "a very deep, still, soul-quiet." There is a proverb to the effect that muddy water, if allowed to be still for a while, becomes clear. So with the psyche. The turmoil simmers down, if one waits, puts aside distractions, and listens. To one long accustomed to the humdrum orientation of the materialistic world, it may not at first "feel right." But gradually, from the mists there emerges some individual, personalized variation of the greatest story ever told by man and through him—a cosmic serial story, forever adding new installments.

It begins in prehistory, perhaps ten thousand years ago, when some half-savage tribesmen got the idea that the principle back of creation was a personal force, and that "it"—or rather "He"—had spoken to them. When asked who he was he replied, "I Am Who I Am." It was not much to go on, but they accepted the deal—"covenant"—he offered, a kind of evolutionary partnership. A majority, including the sophisticated elite, inclined to pooh-pooh. But those who listened heard. The same voice has spoken from generation to generation, epoch to epoch, until now it speaks to our own time, to me, and, if you choose to listen, to you.

Though these exalted historical facts are valuable background for a first approach, as practical people we must not be disappointed if the gates of "heaven" do not swing open at the first discordant blast of our new bugle. Many people quite unrealistically believe that meditation is going to result at once in marvelous paranormal or occult experiences. It may do exactly that, but also it may not. We must be prepared, as all the great ones have been, for the long haul.

At the opposite extreme, some believe that they must discipline their bodies until they are under complete and perfect control before meditation can be successful. But we who live in the Western world do not have the leisure and usually even the will to engage in prolonged periods of meditation, or to submit to the rigid disciplines of the Yogin of India and the medieval Christian mystics. For us, it must suffice to use in the best way possible what time is available to us. But our effort must be consistent.

Twenty minutes to half an hour a day may be sufficient. It doesn't matter when you do it; time means nothing in a spiritual sense. Sometimes I cannot find the time really to meditate into the silence—get acquainted with myself and take stock of what's going on—until just before I go to bed. Sometimes I go to sleep while I am detached and have my mind focused on some problem for which somebody has asked help. The subconscious mind takes over and in the morning I quite often have an answer. In that way I have been able to help many people I have never seen, but who are desperately in need of help.

Each beginner should find a place where it is as quiet as it is possible to be in this noisy world. He should shut out as much light as possible and sit in the most comfortable position he can. When I was studying with Yogan-

anda we always sat on the floor, because that is the traditional way in the East, where chairs until recently have
been very scarce. Most of us are not adept in the strange
postures some of the Yogins can manage, but if you have
experimented with such positions—"asanas"—and like
them, by all means use them. If you have not found the
squatting position difficult there is some advantage in it.
It relaxes the whole body, and thus helps toward the end
purpose of meditation.

Yogananda taught us that if you start early enough and
can manage the asanas, well and good. If you have other
means of keeping your body in shape you may use other
positions. The important thing is to have the spine perfectly straight, and this is best managed by many by simply
lying flat on the floor.

Next, choose something to meditate *about*. Concentration is the first lesson, and an essential for further progress.
To concentrate means to bring the mind to one-pointed
condition. This requires an object of concentration. Some
people find it difficult or impossible, in the beginning, to
use any abstract concept as their object of concentration.
These may achieve success by concentrating on a simple
physical object—a ring, a pencil, a rose, a spoon. I know
one man who was successful using as his object of meditation a remote lake he once saw, high in a far-away moun-
tain valley. Another person, finding abstract concepts no
obstacle, meditated on the saying, "Love God with all your
heart, mind, strength and soul." Whatever one chooses as
object of meditation, the important thing is to stay with it
without deviation until one is deeply, perhaps totally in
empathy with it. When this happens the workaday mind
and body are at rest and out of the way, and the subliminal
consciousness can come into play.

If you are hoping to establish contact with discarnates it
is best to choose someone in the spirit world you love,

have known well, who has meant a great deal to you, and whom you can visualize with no effort. Yogananda used to teach that it is much easier if you concentrate on a thing or person who has meaning to you, one that evokes an emotional response in you. If you are interested to have the cooperation of discarnates they will cooperate if you ask them to. If you are interested in that kind of contact, visualize someone you really love. See him clearly before you, with your eyes closed. See him, visualize him, meanwhile breathing deeply to the count of about eight. Breathe in through the nostrils. Don't force it. Just breathe deeply. Then exhale to the count of seven or eight. Always exhale through the mouth.

Because so much nonsense has been written about breathing, I am leaving out the Sanskrit and Hindi words. There is no need to encumber ourselves with a lot of mystical and occult terms—there are difficulties enough without adding to them. The important thing about breathing is to establish the rhythm; it makes it easier to achieve detachment. As you breathe in you will find after a short time the person you are visualizing will seem to ride your breath in and be closer. As you exhale through the mouth he will recede. This is purely a subjective exercise, to bring back into use the spiritual muscles that have lost their strength—just as the physical muscles of your arm would if you bound it to your side for a year. We have become so enmeshed in external affairs that it is hard for us to attend to subjective matters.

Ultimately, the thing you are visualizing, if the "thing" is a person, will begin to take on life. It will respond to your desires. You will have the feeling as you inhale and exhale that you are swaying back and forth. Your body will seem suspended. You will be in an almost hypnotic mood.

Don't be afraid of the term "self-hypnosis." Hypnosis simply means sleep. As Stanley Hall reminds us, all spiritual and religious disciplines are hypnotic in the sense that they are efforts to plant into the subconscious certain ideas that are bigger, loftier, more meaningful, and more useful than the ones we customarily act upon. Once your concern with external matters and concern about personal feelings are out of the way it becomes possible for nobler ideas to take root. The object of concentration is never as important as the degree of concentration, the intensity. Some people balk at going into anything like a hypnotic state because of fear they won't come out of it. Such fear, as any competent psychologist will assure you, is groundless so long as no unfavorable outside forces are present. The person under normal hypnosis, when left alone, simply wakes up when he is ready.

Once a breathing rhythm is established, one may experiment with slowing it down, gradually to half the beginning frequency. If you hold your breath for a second or two—no longer—your mind will be held, too. You will ultimately achieve the kind of suspension that indicates successful concentration. Don't be frightened if you seem to be floating away from your body. This may become a temptation and then an insuperable obstacle. I knew a man who was well on his way to successful meditation when the thought, "My God, this is *scary!*" overtook him. He abandoned his search and has not as yet taken it up again. Don't try to imitate others. Don't clutter your mind with magical incantations. Let your breathing carry you in the deepest meditation. Practice the exercises in your own home every day. You will soon see you have not relinquished control. With this knowledge your fear of deep meditation will pass and the new dimension will begin to open to you.

There is not only safety in numbers, but also spiritual reinforcement and encouragement. If there is a Spiritual Frontiers Fellowship in your community, join it and, if you are serious about these matters, become active in its development group. If not, contact a local clergyman about the possibility of forming a local SFF group. The SFF headquarters, 800 Custer Avenue, Evanston, Ill., 60202, will assist. If this proves impossible—if you are the only one in your area seriously interested in psychic development, attend the church of your choice regularly—even if you do not share all the views of the presiding clergyman. The religious atmosphere in itself has spiritual potency, and regular exposure to it is protective.

If you find a group, go into it quietly and expectantly. Avoid conversation. Each one in the group should do exactly what he has been doing at home. After half an hour have each one tell anything he has seen or felt during the meditation. Meditation should be consistently on the one thing you chose as your object of meditation in the beginning. You are establishing a contact with a power greater than yourself. You are becoming aware of events in another dimension. You may begin to see clairvoyantly or hear clairaudiently. You may slip into trance and say things which will have no meaning for you but which someone in the group may excitedly pronounce evidential. Group meetings should always end with a healing meditation for someone who stands in clear need of healing.

Healing through prayer is, of course, one of the classic spiritual gifts. Prayer, as we have seen, is a form of telepathy. It can become so intense—so charged with love and concern—that it can be transmuted into psychokinesis, the term used to describe the action of mind upon matter. It can thus affect living tissue even at a distance. The secret of spiritual healing is to speak to the condition of the one being healed, to visualize his condition as it is and as it should be, to free the telekinetic energy to effect the favorable change. You do not create this power, you only focus and direct it.

A word about asceticism. The old idea of the holy hermit, sometimes taking the form of monasticism, is still strong in both the Eastern and the Western religious traditions. I take the position that these practices—sometimes translated into "civilian" life as extreme denial of sexual or gustatory appetite—are seldom beneficial and sometimes definitely destructive. St. Jerome once took refuge in a monastery in an effort to achieve the contemplative life. The emptiness of the monastic pattern and the inanities of the professional hermits shattered his nerves and disturbed his mind. After a good try, he returned to the routines of ordinary life.

There are always shining exceptions, of course, but in general the ascetic monastic life has not proved a successful approach to spiritual development. Sometimes, when monks and nuns alternate monastery routine with active ministry to the needs of the outer world—as preachers, teachers, nurses, or administrators—the worst evils of the system are mitigated. I have spent considerable time— sometimes remaining in the monastic routine many weeks —within Western monasteries and Eastern ashrams. There was little indication of spiritual advancement and much evidence of spiritual retardation. There has been rampant sexuality thinly disguised, such as spontaneous ejaculation during devotions. In the effort to sublimate or eliminate perfectly normal biological necessity a person can become obsessed with the very thing he seeks to kill. I have seen, within monastery walls, hypocrisy, jealousy, quarreling, extreme neuroticism, and a most unseemly lack of that brotherly spirit that is supposed to be the goal. Even the Roman Catholic Church is beginning to question the whole principle of celibacy. A sampling survey conducted by a Catholic group called the National Association for Pastoral Renewal reported that more than seven hundred men left the priesthood during 1966 and 1967, half of them to be married. The situation is such, reported the Association, as to demand "a public, fully financed study by the American bishops."

I can find no justification for extreme asceticism, either in personal experience and observation, or in my reading and reflection, or in religious precept. Jesus followed a rhythm Arnold Toynbee has aptly termed "withdrawal and return." Sometimes, we are told, he would "retire unto himself," in meditation. At other times, to use his own words, he "came eating and drinking." There is no evidence that he ever married, but ample evidence that he enjoyed the company of women. Not only did he order a busy entry into the hustle and bustle of the market place for those who followed him, but he hit the dusty road and was content with the sweating crowd himself.

One cannot, of course, lead a life of spiritual growth and at the same time indulge any of the natural appetites to excess. I found that out once and for all in my encounters with drugs and alcohol! But, if one has succeeded in escaping the trap of physical addiction, all the normal drive and appetites find their legitimate places in a balanced order of life. The world is our monastery. The effort to demonstrate spiritual principles in that world is our monastic discipline.

Proving that such demonstrations are regularly possible has been one of the most satisfying aspects of my work. I cite two of my most gifted pupils, Clem Tamburrino and Ted Swager, as examples. In the spring of 1963, Swager was a junior at the Wesley Theological Seminary in Washington. Dr. Edward W. Bauman, who had recently undergone the dramatic "conversion" previously described, was a professor at the seminary as well as pastor of a large church. Bauman was holding group meetings for meditation. Swager attended one night and was told by the visiting medium that he had psychic ability. Bauman gave him my autobiography, *Nothing So Strange*. The next year he joined a Baltimore unit of Spiritual Frontiers Fellowship and had his first sitting with me during one of my visits to that city. Fletcher reaffirmed Swager's psychic ability and suggested that he concentrate on his healing gift, which was very great.

By this time Swager had already begun to demonstrate his powers. A boy in a Baltimore hospital could not have a necessary tonsillectomy because of a long-continued high fever which medication had not been able to control. After a healing service the fever subsided. A singer with a node on the vocal chord was anticipating an operation to have it removed. After a healing session with Swager the operation was called off—the node was gone. Swager had also begun to produce verifiable communications while in trance.

In October of 1967 I visited the church where Swager was by this time pastor, Calvary Methodist in Waldorf, Maryland. "That evening," Swager has written me, "was the turning point in my ministry and in my life." He now began regular Friday and Saturday trips to see me in Philadelphia for advanced instruction. On one of these trips he met another of my recent and most promising discoveries, Clem Tamburrino.

I first met Tamburrino, an armored-truck guard who was then suffering constantly from what was considered an "incurable" back injury, in October of 1964, when he came to my Philadelphia apartment by appointment. Fletcher told him he had the healing gift; I assured him that, since Fletcher was more likely to be right than wrong in such matters, he'd do well to develop his powers. But first, I suggested, he'd better meet my friends Ambrose and Olga Worrall, the famous Baltimore healers, to see what could be done about his back.

"A cloud of pain seemed to rise from me," Tamburrino

has written me. With his health restored to normal, Tamburrino now began developing his own healing abilities in earnest. He began to work with me intensively on meditative techniques, and in a short time had developed reliable powers of clairvoyance and clairaudience. Then one evening during a sitting with me Fletcher announced that Clem was ready to begin his healing work. His first three cases were people who were in desperate straits either mentally or physically. One was suicidal. His success with these three convinced him.

Tamburrino gives all the days he is not riding his truck to healing, for which he accepts no pay. Among his documented successes are these: A woman, wife of a nationally syndicated newspaper columnist, who had suffered from emphysema for fifteen years and had become an advanced case. Her condition has been dramatically improved. I sent him a brilliant young man of twenty-three whose life was being ruined by something doctors had diagnosed as cerebral palsy. His hand shook so violently that he could not hold a pencil, much less a job. Tamburrino rediagnosed his problem as neurosis and healed him. The young man passed an employment test with top scores and now has a good job.

These two, Swager and Tamburrino, began to develop their psychic abilities by the methods suggested in this chapter. They are only two among many. But their natural gifts are great. They will be heard from.

Scientists Please Note

12

The intent of this book is to bring to public notice the fact that we have been incompletely and sometimes mistakenly informed about the nature and structure of human life and of the universe. Since this is an age of science, the public looks to scientists for verification of new and unfamiliar ideas; to convince the public one must first convince the scientists.

The average scientist is not easily moved to consider unfamiliar evidence. Important innovators (Galileo, Leeuwenhoek, Freud, Salk) sometimes find heavy going. Psychic events, occurring as they do at their own whim, deny the scientist one of his cherished rituals, the experiment repeatable at will. For this reason, many refuse to confront the events and substitute rhetoric for research. Some, however, *have* examined the evidence, which has now accumulated to a point where any scientist still clinging to orthodox materialism is dangerously unscientific and out of date. A growing number of influential scientists who know this are becoming daily more concerned to arouse those who don't.

Dr. Joseph Mayer struck the keynote in a paper read at

a meeting of the American Association for the Advancement of Science.

Have not mechanism and materialism intimidated the world of scholarship long enough? Is it not time academicians stopped using the word "spirit" apologetically, furtively, or in a whisper? If one wishes to assert his faith in "matter," now thought to be somewhat indeterminately composed of empty space interspersed with whirling particle-like events, as a "firm base for the exploration of reality," he is of course at liberty to do so. But should one not likewise feel completely free these days to assert his faith in a "mentalistic" or "spiritualistic" hypothesis, either in opposition to or in conjunction with the materialistic view?

One can readily perceive some respects in which human activity runs parallel to the new physics. If particle-like events lack material substance, so do the things of the mind. If complete continuity seems absent in the sub-atomic world, this is not particularly strange, for the stream of human consciousness is broken when a man sleeps and it is only memory (another present enigma) that holds his experiences together. Man's immediate memory makes him aware of emotion, perception, desire, anticipation, decision, fulfillment. Are the rudiments of these also discernible or inferable at lower levels of consciousness, and in particle-like events themselves? Possibly science will find answers to these questions as it matures. At any rate, the freedom and emergent creation we feel in ourselves are no longer foreign to atomic physics or to modern cosmology. May it not be that a fuller understanding of the new outlook now made necessary will lift men and nations out of their despair and give them renewed faith and confidence? Materialism has never been completely scientific. It is a

Nobel Prize-winning physicist, Professor Percy W. Bridgman of Harvard, who said, "We stand on the threshold of a new era of human thought."[1]

An impressive number of Nobel Prize-winning physicists have accepted this new, more liberal interpretation of their professional obligations. Professor Arthur H. Compton frequently spoke on scientific insights that gave belief in immortality a strong position as a scientific possibility. Dr. Wolfgang Pauli has recently taken up experiments in Europe to explore the narrowing no-man's-land between things mental and things physical. Dr. Richard Feynman of the California Institute of Technology, Nobel Prize-winner for physics in 1965, has been quoted as comparing the universe to "a hierarchy, with ranks from the simplest atomic structure to the most subtle concepts of mind, reaching toward comprehension of God."[2] Even mathematics, "queen and servant of science," bends toward the spiritual. Since Godel's Theorem of 1933 demonstrated that no mathematical system can be proved consistent within itself, mathematicians have been less rigidly materialistic. "Mathematics," a distinguished practitioner of the art has written, "is based on faith."

"Science has found that nothing can disappear without a trace," writes Wernher von Braun, recipient of the Smithsonian Institution's 1967 Langley Award. "Nature does not know extinction; all it knows is transformation. Everything science has taught me, and continues to teach me, strengthens my belief in the continuity of our spiritual existence after death."[3] The professor who writes as "N. Emorey" foresees an eventual coalition of all the specialties concerned to comprehend the universe we live in, and finds this "not surprising, in the light of current evolution theory."

Religion and science have the same source—man's fascination with the cosmos in which he is involved. The early priests, postulating an earth-mother and sun-father who gave life, were only saying in poetic terms what the modern scientist says when he points out that man's sustenance derives from materials provided by the earth and activated by the sun. The ecstatic zeal that possesses the consecrated saint and the dedicated scientist grows from one root: the glowing, awed awareness of being part of and agents for powers transcending self and giving shape and meaning to a cosmos. A conscious effort of the intellectual community to show the productive link between science and religion would free great quantities of psychic energy for creative evolutionary use. It could end some of the frustrations of millions of pupils who hear what they learned on Sunday laughed to scorn on Monday. It could lift the confusion of adult millions by assuring them that everyone who strives creatively to evolve his own conscious awareness is participating in a significant cosmic event. There have been times in history when the most important contribution of the intellectual was to emphasize differences and define them with precision. The present is not such a time. The need of now is to heal a technology-splintered world by pointing out those things within the cultural attitudes of informed men which are the same.[4]

In the light of the rivalry between United States and Soviet scientists, it is interesting to note that Russian official science has taken cognizance of this vital field. In 1932 the Institute for Brain Research was assigned to study telepathy, somewhat in the manner of the American J. B. Rhine. In 1963 L. L. Vasiliev's book *Experiments in Mental Suggestion* was translated from Russian into English. In discussing telepathy Vasiliev says, "Should one

accept telepathic phenomena as definitely true? One thing
is obvious: they can no longer be ignored, they must be
studied."[5]

So far I have discussed mainly the physical scientists.
An equal or possibly even greater hold on popular credulity
is exercised by the behavioral sciences. Currently the most
influential of these is psychology, and the greatest name
in psychology is Freud. Here we must distinguish sharply
between Freud and orthodox Freudians. It is practically
certain that the discarnate Freud does not identify with
this group. The Swiss psychiatrist Carl Jung, who attended
carefully to psychic phenomena all his life, had been a
close professional associate of Freud. After their formal
professional break in 1911, a cordial relationship was resumed and maintained by correspondence. In a letter
written by Freud to Jung in the spring of 1909, Freud airily
dismissed Jung's "investigations of the spook-complex" as
a "lovely delusion," and expressed the hope that Jung
would soon return to the solid paths trod by more sensible
men. Some time during the next two years Freud under-
went some kind of deep, soul-changing experience. On
June 15, 1911, he wrote Jung as follows: ". . . In matters
of the occult I have become humble ever since the great
lesson I received from Ferenczi's experiences. I promise
to believe everything that can be made to seem the least
bit reasonable. As you know, I do not do so gladly. But my
hubris has been shattered. I should like to have you and
F. acting in consonance when one of you is ready to take
the perilous step of publication, and I imagine this would
be quite compatible with complete independence during
the progress of the work. . . .

Cordial regards . . .

Your faithful

Freud"[6]

Freud's reference to publication as a "perilous step"
indicates a hostility to innovation manifested by rank-and-

file members of the intellectual establishment that is reminiscent of Galileo's experience with his suggestions about the solar system. A great many present-day scientists who are not only fully aware of the flaws in the materialistic hypothesis, but themselves possess psychic gifts, are reluctant to have their talents be publicly known because to do so would be professionally "perilous." Dr. Karagulla has found this attitude of mind a constant impediment to her studies. Herself a member of the scientific community, she has become a kind of unofficial clearing-house for information about psychically talented scientists. Many of these are careful, writes Dr. Karagulla, "not to let their gifts be known."[7]

The cure for scientific obstinacy is, of course, direct experience. Dr. Robert A. Bradley, a physician, recently told of his own "conversion experience" in these terms.

Arising before anyone else one morning, I descended the stairs of our big old house and strolled into the empty dining room to use the heavily-weighted lighter that was resting on the marble-topped table. As my hand approached it, I was startled to see the lighter gently rise and float about a foot away, coming silently to rest on its side. In bewilderment I examined it minutely. There were no strings attached, and all the other occupants of the house were still upstairs sleeping. I noticed that when deliberately tipped over, no matter how slowly it was pushed off balance, the lighter would fall noisily with a metallic clink, not silently.

One often reads of similar, unexplained physical happenings occurring to others and dismisses them with a shrug of skepticism. Surely, one says, these happenings can be traced to hallucinations, practical jokes, trickery, fraud, etc. But let it happen to you. Just *once* let it happen to you![8]

The cigar-lighter episode was only the beginning of a series of events that convinced Dr. Bradley that the universe contains powers not apprehended either by our conventional five senses or by any presently known instrumentation.

Most of the examples of psychic phenomena so far mentioned in this book describe *kinds* of manifestations of the psychic power known for many centuries and often observed under the very strictest of scientific conditions. The fact that these manifestations readily adapt themselves to new conditions adds an additional facet to the whole matter. Photography, as historic time goes, is a fairly recent development. Some years ago, while on a visit to Chicago, some friends of mine who were interested in every kind of psychic phenomenon introduced me to a young man named Ted Serios, a bellhop. Serios, it was said, could "think" pictures onto unexposed photographic film with such force that, when developed, the film was found to bear the mentally transmitted picture as if it had been normally exposed.

I witnessed several days of demonstrations by Serios during which every conceivable protection against fraud was taken—picking up film and cameras at stores randomly selected, allowing him to handle the camera only briefly, watching closely, and so on. After many months of demonstrations for the press, for qualified researchers, and for the curious, Serios was taken over by Dr. Jules Eisenbud, a psychoanalyst and psychic investigator, for a methodical series of tests which finally resulted in a book.[9] Serios simply holds the camera with the lens pointed toward himself, goes into a light trance, and "projects" his picture. He has produced a great variety of pictures, some of which have been reproduced in the press. These include views of the Eiffel Tower, President Kennedy, an Egyptian Pharaoh, and numerous architectural effects, some of them made in compliance with special requests. Though I did not know it at the time, other psychics were doing psycho-photography in other parts of the world.[10]

How many possess this gift? The Eastman Kodak Company has had exhibitions of "thought photography" for some time. The repeated discovery, through routine personnel work in places where film is manufactured and processed, of people who must be excluded from this kind of work because they fog film in handling it, is taken as an indication that many have potential psychophotographic ability. Dr. Karagulla reports a psychic who can impress pictures directly on sealed film without the aid of a camera or any other device.

Water-dowsing, one of the most ancient of the mediumistic arts still to be routinely practiced, is commonplace in rural sections. Recently, however, it bobbed up in one of the most erudite communities of one of the biggest cities in the world. During the 1966 drought in the East, municipal restrictions on the use of water put Columbia University's athletic fields in danger of becoming dust bowls. Unless some other source of water could be found, no turf could be grown on them. A government hydrologist and a well-drilling concern were called in and eight test-drillings were put down. All were dry. By this time one of the university's Ph.D.s had had enough of such folderol and, "perilous" or not, unmasked himself. He was a water-witch, a dowser; his name, Dr. George J. Halasi-Kun. He took a brass rod, paced back and forth over the dry field noting where the rod dipped, indicated two spots and said "drill here." Both locations produced abundant water.[11]

In February of 1968 (under auspices of the Spiritual Frontiers Fellowship) the Rev. Norman Evans of Camden, N.J., a well-known dowser who can direct searchers to water without himself being on the scene, gave a lecture featuring audience participation at the Riverside Church in New York. Using various wooden, nylon, and metallic implements, including coathangers, members of the audience passed over a water main Evans had correctly predicted would be found running under the hall. Several members of the audience discovered for the first time that they had the gift. The novelist Kenneth Roberts has described the work of another famous dowser.[12]

One of the much-debated passages in the New Testament is that which describes Jesus' telekinetic withering of the fig tree. Always remembering that any theological evaluation of Jesus does not depend upon his unquestioned and preeminent psychic ability, we may ask whether any comparable psychic effect is being demonstrated today. It is. John Kobler reported one such instance in his article, already cited, in the *Saturday Evening Post* for March 9, 1968. The "psychic" in this case is a lie-detector expert named Cleve Backster. Kobler quotes Backster as follows:

> I was watering a plant in my office when I began wondering how long it takes the moisture to rise from the roots to the leaves. The psychic galvanic reflex in a polygraph machine measures the changes in body conductivity. Why not try it on the plant? I attached the electrodes to both sides of a leaf, expecting the line on the chart to go up as the water rose. It went down instead. I'd never seen that kind of reaction in people *unless some kind of emotion was involved.*
>
> When humans are threatened, the polygraph gives a sharp reaction. I decided to threaten the plant's well-being. I dipped a leaf into a cup of coffee. Nothing happened. I tried music. Not a flicker. Finally I thought, "I'll burn the damn thing." It was just a thought, but the polygraph pen leaped. I got some matches and made passes at the plant. Wild excitement. For months

I observed different plants. They reacted to all sorts of strange activity. When I brought in my dog, up went the polygraph pen.

Backster then speculated on how the troubles of other species would affect the plants. He got some live shrimp and killed them by dumping them into hot water. The recording pen leaped frantically. Could it be that when cell life dies it sends out a signal picked up by other cells?

I noticed that if something more interesting than shrimp distracted the plants they wouldn't react, so I gave them plenty to worry about. I introduced shock conditioning à la Pavlov. Then I set my apparatus so that when the first shrimp dropped into the hot water the plants would get an electrical charge, but there'd be none with the next shrimp. Still, they'd react as if shocked. After a while I had only to think about shocking them and they'd go into coma like a person fainting.

Is it unreasonable to suggest that this kind of thing contains a possibility for discovery even more far-reaching than that of Einstein, whose curiosity was provoked by "insignificant" but persistent perturbations in the orbit of Mercury? Does Mr. Backster's work suggest anything to our established science of biology? Is it not proper to expect of science a conscientious attempt to interpret phenomena in such a way as to give us something like a coherent world? Is it, indeed, altogether *honorable* to neglect, decade after decade, data that have established their authenticity and await interpretation? Yet the psychical world abounds with instances of such neglect. Let me mention just one more example, the phenomenon of psychometry, or "object-reading." I cite an instance from my own work, a sitting which took place on March 10,

1967. The transcript of what happened while I was in trance is by the sitter, V. Roth, whom I had not previously known.

My sitting took place in Philadelphia. I had never had a sitting with any other medium. I had been referred to Mr. Ford by Dr. W. G. Roll of the Psychical Research Foundation, Durham, N.C.

After handing Fletcher, through Mr. Ford, a thimble I thought had belonged to my late grandmother, he described her background and gave one of her initials —all incorrectly. My mother later verified that the thimble had been sent by a woman, now deceased, who had been a close friend of my grandmother. My mother and father both verified the complete accuracy of Fletcher's description of this woman.

I handed Fletcher, by way of Mr. Ford, an article that had belonged to my uncle. Fletcher correctly identified our relationship, place of residence and the cause of my uncle's death. . . . Suddenly a voice spoke through Mr. Ford with the identical accent and inflection of my uncle's speech. I felt as though I'd been kicked in the stomach! The particular words spoken had always been a private joke between us.

"Is it James?" Fletcher asked. I always called my uncle "Jim," but he always referred to himself as "James." If Fletcher had "taken" the name from my mind it would have been "Jim," but if from my uncle's mind it would have been "James," which of course it was. When I asked for evidence that it really was Jim, Fletcher asked if the name "Raymond" meant anything to me, in connection with working in radio or TV. At the time it didn't, but later five different people verified the fact that years ago, without my knowing, Jim had lived on Raymond Avenue and worked for RCA.

Psychometry is an ancient phenomenon still without explanation by scientists or by anyone else, beyond the facts that objects carry their own histories with them somewhat as persons carry their memories, and that certain people are able under certain conditions to perceive these histories. Ruth Montgomery reports another instance.

Though Ford is primarily a trance medium rather than a psychometrist, I once handed him a pocket watch and asked him if he could tell me anything about its ownership. He held it between the palms of his hands for a few minutes and then began to massage his arms as if they ached. "The watch belonged to your father," he said. "He suffered with pains that shot down his arms from the shoulders to his hands. I know; I am picking up his agony." In his later years, Dad would often get up at night and run hot water over his arms and hands to ease the frightful pain for which his doctors had no cure. Since only our immediate family know this, Ford could not have known it by normal means.

This book has by no means completed the cataloguing of the *kinds* of events that have repeated themselves decade after decade, century after century, without the scientists after the "Enlightenment" taking serious and collective notice. There is Therese Neumann, a physically substantial woman who lived a lifetime without taking significant amounts of food, water, or substitute physical nutrients.[13] There is Father Pio, who has both levitated and made appearances at points far distant from his physical body. There is the gravity-defying practice of table-tilting, a parlor pastime for many American and European families. There is the fact that Fletcher has brought messages in languages, including Chinese, Hindi, and Arabic, that neither he nor I had ever known. There is, in fact, an overwhelming accumulation of evidence that things which, by any standard theory of the structure of the physical universe, could not possibly happen, are in fact regularly happening. Am I too forward in suggesting that perhaps a new and more imaginative concept of the universe is long overdue?

Of course I am not alone in asking this question. One of the other questioners was brought to my attention with particular force by sheer circumstance. When I published my autobiography *Nothing So Strange* in 1958 it was given by the *Saturday Review* to Siegfried Mandel for review. Mandel, troubled by what he had read, first attended one of my seances, then wrote his review, which concluded:

It was a two-way exchange that produced signs of recognition, puzzlement and amazement in the seventeen listeners, among them doctors, the mayor of a large city, newspapermen, a movie star and a minister. When Fletcher addressed me, I greeted him politely, and in turn a series of persons I had known made comments and remarks so personal that my hair stood on end. I tried to account for this strange demonstration in several ways, but had to reject hypnosis, telepathy, psychological guesswork, trickery, research and photographic memory. I filled a notebook with reactions and stories by the other participants after the session was over and was unable to find inconsistencies of clues that would cast doubt. . . . We may have in the psychic field elements that will find scientific interpretation. Until such time, these exploratory experiences give us food for thought.[14]

The vernal equinox moves through a complete zodiacal sign in approximately two thousand years. Thus the "first point of Aries" moved into Pisces, where it has been for nearly two millennia, and is about to enter Aquarius. This is taken astrologically to indicate major historical epochs, and here even nonastrological historians support the case. The Babylonian civilization was born about 4000 B.C.; the Greco-Roman sequence began about 2000 B.C.; Western Christendom was born about 0 B.C. or A.D. In each case the spring point was entering a new sign of the zodiac.

Pisces, the sign of the fishes, has ruled the Christian Era, and the fish has been a Christian symbol from the very beginning of Christianity. The next sign, Aquarius, is defined as "characteristic of a persistent effort to stabilize the the values of living by an adequate realization of life's meaning."[15] This may be taken, astrologically speaking, as a statement of the main task of the post-year-2000 world now in the process of being born. It doesn't take an astrologer (which I am not) to see that such a program would make a good deal of sense.

"An adequate realization of life's meaning." We can hardly misread the signs of the times. Modern physics, when pushed to its frontiers, always tends to run over into metaphysics. In the search for truth there is nothing to be hid, nothing to be evaded or ignored or glossed over. Our age offers opportunities for the splendid minds, the superb training, the deep intuitions of science to discover and verify the unknown universes within reach. Scientists have the public ear as never before; they can help usher in a new age, more varied, more interesting, more exciting than anything ever known. Let the scientific mind, therefore, be truly scientific. Let it explore. Let it help mankind to understand and to live out its destiny.

Notes

CHAPTER 1

1. *Nothing So Strange* (New York, 1958).

CHAPTER 2

1. St. Clair Stobart, *Torchbearers of Spiritualism* (London, 1925).
2. Anonymous, *Alcoholics Anonymous* (New York, 1939).
3. Fabre d'Olivet, *Hermeneutic Interpretation* (Paris, 1820).
4. G. Maurice Elliott, *The Psychic Life of Jesus* (London, 1964).
5. G. Maurice Elliott, *The Bible as Psychic History* (London, 1959); Gertrude Ogden Tubby, *Psychics and Mediums* (Boston, 1935).
6. Jean Burton, *Heyday of a Wizard* (New York, 1944); Hereward Carrington, *The Psychic World* (London, 1937).
7. John Kobler, "ESP," *Saturday Evening Post*, March 9, 1968.
8. Ruth Montgomery, *A Search for the Truth* (New York, 1967).

9. J. B. Rhine and J. G. Pratt, *Parapsychology* (Springfield, Ill. and Oxford, Eng., 1957).
10. *New York Times,* May 22, 1968.
11. John Sherrill, *They Speak with Other Tongues* (New York, 1964).

CHAPTER 3

1. Leslie D. Weatherhead, *After Death* (New York, 1936).
2. Casper S. Yost, "The Coming of Patience Worth," in *The Psychic Source Book,* Alson J. Smith, ed. (New York, 1951).
3. Carrington, *op. cit.*
4. In *You Will Survive After Death* (New York, 1950).
5. See *The Psychic Source Book,* noted above.
6. Thomas Sugrue, *There Is a River* (New York, 1942).
7. See Josephine Lucas Johnson, *The Mysteries of the Space Age* (New York, 1966).

CHAPTER 4

1. "Sittings with Arthur Ford," a compilation from the Spiritual Frontiers Fellowship.
2. Sugrue, *op. cit.*
3. Eddy, *op. cit.* (chap. 3, n. 4).
4. Carrington, *op. cit.*
5. *The Psychic Source Book.*
6. *Tomorrow* magazine (Autumn 1957).
7. Shafica Karagulla, M.D., *Breakthrough to Creativity* (Los Angeles, 1967).

CHAPTER 5

1. Robert Crookall, *Intimations of Immortality* (London, 1965).
2. *Ibid.*
3. *Ibid.*

4. 2 Cor 12:2.
5. 1 Cor 15:44.
6. Crookall, *op. cit.*
7. Karagulla, *op. cit.*
8. G. N. M. Tyrrell, *Grades of Significance* (London, 1931).

CHAPTER 6

1. Tyrrell, *op. cit.*

CHAPTER 7

1. George Lawton, *The Drama of Life After Death* (New York, 1932).

CHAPTER 8

1. Louis K. Anspacher, *The Challenge of the Unknown* (New York, 1947).
2. *Ibid.*
3. "Sittings . . . ," *op. cit.*
4. Montgomery, *op. cit.*

CHAPTER 9

1. Private communication to author.
2. Stewart Edward White, *The Unobstructed Universe* (New York, 1940).
3. Richard Maurice Bucke, *Cosmic Consciousness* (New York, 1901).
4. London, 1916.
5. New York, 1937.
6. *Op. cit.*
7. New York, 1942.

CHAPTER 10

1. Kobler, *op. cit.*
2. "Why Is Astrology So Popular?" *Christian Herald* (May, 1966).

3. A more extended version of the Sun Myung Moon sittings, containing some special illumination on points of Christian faith, may be obtained by writing Walter Voelker, 950 Wellington Road, Elkins Park, Pa. 19117.

CHAPTER 11

1. Sermon, Southwark Cathedral, November 3, 1963.
2. From 1 Cor 12, 13, New English Bible.

CHAPTER 12

1. Section L, AAAS, December 28, 1954, Berkeley, Calif.
2. N. Emorey, *A Serious Call to an American (R)Evolution* (New Haven, 1967).
3. Wernher von Braun, "Immortality," *This Week* magazine, January 24, 1960.
4. Emorey, *op. cit.*
5. Quoted by Karagulla, *op. cit.*
6. C. G. Jung, *Memories, Dreams, Reflections* (New York, 1961).
7. *Op. cit.*
8. Dorothy Bomar Bradley and Robert A. Bradley, M.D., *Psychic Phenomena: Revelations and Experiences* (West Nyack, 1967).
9. Jules Eisenbud, *The World of Ted Serios* (New York, 1967).
10. See Bradley and Bradley, *op. cit.*, and Karagulla, *op. cit.*
11. *New York Times*, September 26, 1966.
12. *Henry Gross and His Dowsing Rod* (New York, 1951).
13. Nandor Fodor, Encyclopaedia of Psychic Science (London, 1933).
14. Siegfried Mandel, "His Man Fletcher," *Saturday Review*, November 11, 1958.
15. Marc Edmond Jones, quoted in "Why Is Astrology So Popular," *op. cit.* (chap. 10, n. 2).

Index

J